30 Days To Confident Leadership

30 Days To Confident Leadership

Bobb Biehl

Nashville, Tennessee

Printed in the United States of America

0-8054-0173-3

Published by Broadman & Holman Publishers,
Nashville, Tennessee
Acquisitions and Development Editor: Vicki Crumpton

Dewey Decimal Classification: 303.3
Subject Heading: LEADERSHIP
Library of Congress Card Catalog Number: 97-35170

Library of Congress Cataloging-in-Publication Data

Biehl, Bobb.
[Increasing your leadership confidence]
30 days to confident leadership / Bobb Biehl.
p. cm.
Originally published : Increasing your leadership confidence. Sisters, OR., Questar Publishers, 1989.
ISBN 0-8054-0173-3 (pb)
1. Leadership. I. Title. II. Title: Thirty days to confident leadership.
HD57.7.B53 1998
658.4'092—dc21

97-35170
CIP

1 2 3 4 5 02 01 00 99 98

CONTENTS

CONTENTS

ELEPHANT STAKES

I once had the privilege of experiencing something every kid dreams of—joining the circus.

Late one Friday night I was sound asleep when the phone rang. The caller was Duane Pederson, founder and editor of the *Hollywood Free Paper,* and a friend of mine. "How would you like to go to Tucson tomorrow?" he said.

"Tucson?" I groaned. "What in the world would we do in Tucson?"

He told me that our friend Bobby Yerkes, who was involved in "Circus of the Stars," was working at a circus performing there the next day. "I'd like to just go down, get away, clear the cobwebs, and work the circus with him. We'll move some props, have a good time, and be back by ten o'clock tomorrow night." It didn't take me long to agree to go.

Early the next morning we flew from Los Angeles to Tucson. It was a hot, dusty, windy day at the fairgrounds where the circus was set up.

We moved props from one ring to the next, helped in any way we could, and generally got dirty, tired, and hungry.

During one of the breaks I started chatting with a man who trained animals for Hollywood movies. "How is it," I asked, "that you can stake down a ten-ton elephant with the same size stake you use for this little fellow?" (The "little fellow" weighed three hundred pounds.)

"It's easy," he answered, "when you know two things: elephants really do have great memories, but they aren't very smart. When they're babies, we stake them down. They try to tug away from the stake maybe ten thousand times before they realize they can't possibly get away. At that point, their 'elephant memory' takes over, and they remember for the rest of their lives that they can't get away from the stake."

We humans are sometimes like these elephants. I've heard many executives tell me that when they were teenagers someone said to them, "You'll never be a leader" or "You're not very quick" or "You never think things through" or "You don't know how to work with people" (or "money" or "numbers") or "You don't communicate well." When we hear those things in our youth, zap! It drives a stake into our minds. Often as adults we still are held back by these inaccurate one-sentence "stakes" embedded in our memories.

As you read *Thirty Days to Confident Leadership,* I hope you'll pull up some of the stakes that are holding you back. You're probably capable of much more than you think you are. You're more mature and capable than you were even twelve months ago, and next year you'll be able to do things you can't do today.

So let's pull up those stakes—and go on together to true leadership confidence!

INTRODUCTION

As president of Masterplanning Group International for the last decade, I've worked with more than a hundred corporate presidents and directors of nonprofit organizations, as well as senior pastors of large churches. I've also worked with more than a thousand board members, executive staff members, and other top executives. As I've worked with them, I've continually asked myself, "What are the common strengths that all outstanding leaders share?"

Of course, any given leader may have a unique strength in this or that area; but what, I asked, are those few common denominators shared by every person I've worked with who's been a confident leader?

As a result of that search, I've identified thirty answers—thirty common denominators. They can be classified in four different types of leadership dimensions:

1. Coping skills that enable a leader to deal effectively with

- ❖ change
- ❖ depression
- ❖ failure
- ❖ fatigue
- ❖ pressure

2. Aspects of growth and maturity—

- ❖ attractiveness
- ❖ balance
- ❖ confidence
- ❖ creativity
- ❖ discipline
- ❖ self-motivation

3. Skills needed when directly responsible for staff members—

- ❖ asking questions
- ❖ communication
- ❖ decision making
- ❖ dreaming
- ❖ goal setting
- ❖ influencing
- ❖ handling money
- ❖ personal organization
- ❖ prioritizing
- ❖ problem solving
- ❖ risk taking

4. Skills a leader needs when he works regularly and directly with a staff—

- ❖ delegating
- ❖ firing
- ❖ masterplanning
- ❖ motivating others
- ❖ people building
- ❖ recruiting
- ❖ reporting
- ❖ team building

These all add up to *thirty leadership aspects*—thirty quite diverse dimensions that are sometimes hard to understand and pull together. But I believe they reflect the essence of leadership, and each one is covered in a chapter all its own in this book.

What is leadership? If you ask the next fifty people you see to define the word *leadership,* I predict you will get at least forty-nine different answers.

About ten years ago I felt it was important for our firm to develop a simple definition of leadership that our whole team could use consistently. So I sat down and spent several hours trying to write a crystal-clear, profoundly simple definition of leadership. Today, after ten years of using that definition, I haven't found a single leadership situation to which it doesn't apply. Here it is.

LEADERSHIP IS

- knowing *what* to do next;
- knowing *why* that's important; and
- knowing *how* to bring appropriate resources to bear on the need at hand.

In any group, whoever supplies the answer to these questions will emerge as the leader of that group, regardless of his or her formal position or how it was obtained (by appointment, election, inheritance, or whatever).

I hope you'll make *Thirty Days to Confident Leadership* a lifelong resource. As a leader, whenever you run into a problem or a tough decision or a challenging communication task, you can always pick up this book and turn right to the section that has specific help for you. It will clarify what to do next and why, and point you toward other resources available.

To make your future reference easier, each chapter in this book is organized under five to ten headings, each of which is a basic question to help you in that chapter's subject area. When you face a tough problem, for example, turn to chapter 26, "Problem Solving," start asking yourself the right questions, and potential solutions will surface in your thinking. When you're analyzing a major risk, turn to chapter 29 on "Risk Taking," ask the right questions, and your perspective on the risk will begin to clear. Simple as that!

As you ask yourself these questions and gain clarity, you'll be a more confident leader of people.

If you ask yourself profound questions, you get profound answers. If you ask yourself shallow questions, you get shallow answers. And, if you ask no questions at all, you get no answers at all.

Before we continue, take a little breather by looking at the leadership evaluation chart on the following page. Where do you fit?

A PERSONAL LEADERSHIP EVALUATION

AREAS OF LEADERSHIP

RATING:	Proficiency & Expertise	Quickness, Responsiveness	Determination & Drive	Versatility, Adaptability	Communication Skills
★★★★★ **Far Exceeds Requirements**	Leaps tall buildings with a single bound.	Is faster than a speeding bullet.	Is stronger than a locomotive.	Walks on water.	Talks with kings.
★★★★ **Exceeds Requirements**	Leaps tall buildings with a running start.	Is as fast as a speeding bullet.	Is as strong as a bull elephant.	Keeps head above water under stress.	Talks with governors.
★★★ **Meets Requirements**	Can leap short buildings if prodded.	Can keep up with a slow bullet.	Is almost as strong as a bull.	Washes with water.	Talks to self.
★★ **Needs Improvement**	Bumps into buildings.	Misfires frequently.	Shoots the bull.	Drinks water.	Argues with self.
★ **Does Not Meet Minimum Requirements**	Cannot recognize buildings.	Wounds self when handling guns.	Smells like a bull.	Passes water in an emergency.	Loses arguments with self.

1 ASKING QUESTIONS

About twenty years ago I decided to make a hobby of asking questions. I began collecting questions, just as some people collect stamps or antiques. As a result, this chapter topic is one of my favorites.

I hope you too will make both collecting and asking questions a lifelong hobby because *questions are essential* to gaining knowledge and understanding.

If you and I could sit down together on a park bench on a sunny spring day and talk for an hour about any situation or problem or risk—anything you're trying to think through and analyze and gain perspective on—what single situation would you want to discuss?

With that situation focused clearly in your mind, let's work through the questions I would ask to help you.

What? Why? When? Who? How? Where? How much?

Rudyard Kipling called them his "six trusted men"—the questions who, what, when, where, why, and how. As a reporter and writer, Kipling was speaking from a journalistic perspective rather than a leadership perspective, but his questions are helpful for us as well—though we might want to ask them in a different order.

Start with *What?* Can you state, in just a sentence, what is the situation you want to think through today?

Why would you like to think it through? Why is it important to you? Why has this situation developed?

When did it start developing? When do you need to solve it? When do you need to deal with it? When do you need to make some changes?

Who are the primary people involved? Who caused the situation? Who is involved with it? Who is the beneficiary of it? Who benefits most? Who takes the brunt of it? Who is most affected by it?

How do we change it? How do we make a difference? How do we bring appropriate resources to bear?

And *Where?* Is space or place even important? Is it important to do it here in town, or maybe in a different state, or at your house or my house? Where should we do it? Whatever we do to correct the situation, how does "where" fit in?

Another important question I always add is *How much?* How much will it take to correct the situation? How much money? How much time? How much energy? What amount of resources will it take?

As you can see, it's impossible to think through any situation effectively without questions. It isn't just hard; it's actually *impossible.* You *must* ask questions like What? Why? When? Who? How? Where? and How much?

That's why the better you become at asking questions, the better you are at thinking through *anything,* anywhere, at any time, for the rest of your life.

Compared to what?

A second line of questioning I would have you consider is "Compared to what?" *Nothing is meaningful without a context.* So what is the context of the situation you are dealing with? What are the comparisons? What other situations are like it? What have you experienced like it before? What are the facts? And how do you compare those facts with facts in other parts of your life?

A person may be happy making five dollars an hour until he learns that someone next to him is making six dollars for doing the same thing. Now he has a different *context* for evaluating his situation.

A senior executive once said to me, "Bobb, we're $50,000 in the red this month." I think he expected me to turn pale, but instead I calmly asked, "Compared to what?"

He answered, "What do you mean, 'Compared to what?' We're $50,000 in the red this month!"

"Well," I said again, "compared to *what?* If you were projected to be $100,000 in the red, then you're actually in great shape now! If you expected to be $50,000 in the red, you're right on target. And if you were supposed to be $100,000 in the black, you're in deep trouble. So . . . *compared to what?*"

At that he answered, "Well, our projection was that we're supposed to be $46,000 in the red."

"Then relax," I said. "What else do you have to talk about today?"

Maybe you too can relax as you gain the perspective of context. What's the context of the situation you're dealing with today—the broader pictures?

For example, what difference will this situation make ten years from now? In other words, what is the *context of time* and how will time affect it?

What is the *context of money?* How much would the problem cost to correct, and how does that amount compare with all the money you made this year, or all the money you'll make in your lifetime?

What's missing?

The third line of questioning focuses on these two words: *What's missing?* Frankly, I believe our education system today fails to teach us this profound question, but leads us instead to be analytical only about what we *see.*

What missing information is making it difficult for you to get a clear understanding of your situation? What facts do you need to gather to help you see it more clearly?

This is one of the hardest questions to remember to ask yourself, but it frequently unlocks solutions for problems that otherwise just can't be solved.

When any situation has you confused, simply asking "What's missing?" often leads to a major breakthrough.

What is the ideal in this situation?

Another question you'll want to use over and over again is "What is the ideal?" It's actually an "ideal" question—it fits nearly everything.

In the situation you're dealing with—what would be the ideal solution? What would be the outcome if everyone involved acted in an ideal manner? If you had the ideal amount of money? The ideal amount of equipment? The ideal facility? The ideal everything? Ideally, what would we have that we don't have now? And how much of that is truly critical?

Develop an insatiable commitment to seeking the ideal. Build this into your thinking so that until you reach the ideal, you will always have a slight dissatisfaction in your mind.

Until you recognize what the ideal is, you don't know precisely the distance between where you are and where you'd like to be or could be.

What would my five closest friends advise me?

If you asked your five closest friends to help you deal with this situation, what advice would they offer? Often, just imagining their response gives you needed perspective.

Mind–Stretcher (Brainstorming) Questions

1. What is the *essence* of this idea (or task or project or department, etc.)—in one word? One sentence? One paragraph?
2. *Why* am I doing what I am doing?
3. What are my five most *fundamental assumptions* (what I believe to be true) about this idea, in priority order?
4. What would I do to accomplish this task if I had just three minutes to do it? three hours? three days? three years? Unlimited time?
5. Where will this idea be in ten years? fifteen? twenty-five? fifty? one hundred? five hundred?
6. What would change if I had only half the current staff? What if I added one or two extra people? What if I added unlimited staff? What would they do, and why?
7. What changes would I make if I had only half the current budget? Twice the budget? Unlimited budget?
8. How can I double the income and cut the costs in half?
9. Which part of the total idea deserves extra funding?
10. Which parts could I drop and not really miss?
11. What's the ultimate "blue-sky" *potential* of this idea?
12. What five things, in priority order, could keep me from realizing the full potential of this idea or project? How can I clear away the roadblocks?
13. What are the greatest strengths, and how can I maximize them?
14. If I had to start over . . . what would I do differently?
15. What if this idea were one hundred times as successful as I plan?

What lingering questions do I have?

By "lingering questions" I mean those that may not seem terribly important but, nevertheless, are on your mind.

Finally, take a look at the many kinds of questions included in the boxed sections in this chapter. They'll stimulate your thinking and help you gain a fresh perspective on the situation that's challenging you. Try these questions out, and see if you don't discover some fresh perspectives.

A postscript: Perhaps the situation we're discussing on the park bench involves some serious doubts you're wrestling with in your life. If so, I pass along to you these words from author Tom Skinner: "I spent a long time trying to come to grips with my doubts, and suddenly I realized that I had better come to grips with what I believe. I have since moved from the agony of questions that I cannot answer to the reality of answers that I cannot escape. And it is a great relief."

TYPES OF QUESTIONS:	FUNCTION	EXAMPLE	HOW TO DEVELOP A QUESTION OF THIS TYPE	STANDARD BASIS OF THIS QUESTION TYPE
PROBLEM-SOLVING QUESTIONS	To find a solution or answer	*Would you marry me?*	Clearly define the problem, then ask questions that probe into the context of the problem and explore possible solutions.	*What? Why? When? Who? Where? How? How much?*
TEACHING QUESTIONS	To teach someone a new insight	*Can you see the advantages of being married?*	Clearly understand the process or concept to be taught, then ask questions that progressively present the logical steps involved.	*What's next?*
MIND-STRETCHER QUESTIONS	To creatively get a new and different outlook on a situation	*What would it really be like to get married?*	Imagine the situation in a context that is different from present reality.	*What if?*
RHETORICAL QUESTIONS	To make a point more emphatically	*"How do I love thee? Let me count . . ."*	Take a statement and pose it as a question, for emphasis.	———
PERSUASIVE QUESTIONS	To convince a person to accept my perspective	*Would you rather marry me or be single and utterly miserable?*	Ask questions that position my perspective in the best light.	———

TYPES OF QUESTIONS:	FUNCTION	EXAMPLE	HOW TO DEVELOP A QUESTION OF THIS TYPE	STANDARD BASIS OF THIS QUESTION TYPE
INNER-SEARCH QUESTIONS	To start the introspection process	*Why would I want to get married?*	Just keep asking "Why?"	*Why? (ten times in a row)*
LOGIC-CHECK QUESTIONS	To keep from making unnecessary mistakes	*Is there any good reason we shouldn't get married?*	Ask questions that focus on basic truths, reasons, values, commitments, larger perspectives.	*What? Why? When? Who? Where? How? How much?*
PRIORITIZING QUESTIONS	To keep defining the most important items or steps	*Which of these three women should I marry?*	Seek and sift out the most important from the many possibilities—ask questions that require the making of choices.	*Which?*
CONVERSATIONAL QUESTIONS	To pass the time of day	*Did you hear that Tom and Sue got married?*	Pick something we could talk about together, and present the topic in question form.	*What? Why? When? Who? Where? How? How much?*
RESEARCH QUESTIONS	To collect basic data	*Are you married?*	Decide what I need or want to know, then simply request that information.	*What? Why? When? Who? Where? How? How much?*

Executive Prioritizers

Questions to Ask . . .

When things start seeming foggy and overwhelming:

- If I could do only three things this year, what would they be?
- Of those three things, which should be done first? next?
- Fifty years from now, when looking back in time, what will I see as this year's most significant accomplishments?
- (For each concern on your mind:) Is finding a solution to this problem a level-one, level-two, or level-three priority?

When you're prioritizing spending decisions:

- If we had to reduce our budget by 50 percent, what would we cut?

When you're deciding what data to seek or keep:

- To do what we *have to do* what do we *have to know?*

When you're targeting problems:

- What are the two or three "land mines" in this situation that could explode and "kill" this project or program?
- What are the three most frequent miscommunications about our work?
- What problems are you struggling with for which you would happily pay 10 percent of your income to find a guaranteed solution?

When meeting someone who may be a key to your future success:

- Where do you see yourself five years from now?
- What are the biggest obstacles you face in reaching your goals?

When you meet a friend you haven't seen in a while (to get past the small talk):

- What's the most meaningful thing that has happened to you since we last met?

Remember

In the future, whenever you're wrestling with a situation in which you need to clear your mind, pick up this book, turn to this chapter, and ask yourself these fundamental questions:

- What? Why? When? Who? How? Where? How much?
- Compared to what?
- What's missing?
- What is the ideal in this situation?
- What would my five closest friends advise?
- What lingering questions do I have?

Just knowing the right questions to ask helps increase your leadership confidence!

2 ATTRACTIVENESS

Are you as attractive as you'd like to be?

If you can answer yes, you're in the minority, and this chapter wasn't written for you. But I'd still ask you to read it, to discover what you can pass on to others who would like to be more attractive than they are, or who at times feel less attractive than they'd like to feel.

Your attractiveness to other people is a mixture of at least these three things: (1) the inner you, (2) the outer you (on which most Americans put the most emphasis), and (3) your dreams.

With these factors in mind, ask yourself the following key questions:

The Inner You

Do I have a positive attitude?

Do you know anyone who's attractive when he or she is gloomy or grouchy? Of course not. No one is, and that includes you and me.

One especially attractive aspect of people with a positive attitude is that they immediately explore optional solutions whenever they confront a problem. Executives particularly appreciate someone on their staff who consistently approaches such a situation by saying, "Here's the problem, but here are a few possible solutions."

Am I self-centered or others-centered?

On the morning of her first day in a new school, my daughter Kimberly came to me with a typical seventh-grade anxiety attack: "Dad, how do I look? What do you think of my new dress? How do you like my hair? What about my shoes? What about this belt? Does this purse match?" and on and on.

"Honey," I said, "sit down for just a minute." I sat her down and asked, "How do you feel right now?"

"Well, Dad, I . . . I'm gonna be late, and I . . . how do I look?"

"Honey," I said again, "how do you *feel* right now?"

"I . . . I feel sort of nervous, and I wonder if people are going to like me. I wonder if I look all right."

I continued: "When the other kids see you, what would you like them to think? What would you like them to say?"

"I'd like them to say, 'I love your dress, your new hairstyle is neat, and I like your shoes,' or whatever."

"Now then," I went on, "how do you think every other girl in your class is going to feel today?"

She paused and answered, "Probably like I do."

"Darling," I said, "if you want to be popular, and if you want to be attractive to the other kids so they always like to see you coming, then simply take the initiative, and treat others exactly like you want them to treat you."

That evening she told me the first day had gone well. "I did it to everyone I met. I told them I liked their dress or something. And then every one of them told me they liked mine as well."

So her needs were met just as theirs were—everyone came out a winner. If you meet Kimberly today, her first comment will be on something she likes about you—your eyes, your hair, your clothing, something. She always starts a conversation with a compliment.

It's an others-centered rather than a self-centered position, and it's a vital ingredient for attractiveness in the inner you. It tells others that you're confident enough in how you look that you can genuinely appreciate their attractiveness. Feeling unattractive is a self-centered feeling. You can overcome that feeling by putting your focus on meeting others' needs before your own. You'll make more friends as you become a friend to many.

Do I really love people?

Art DeMoss made famous the advice, "Love people and use things—don't love things and use people."

Genuine love for others is a critical component of attractiveness. Why? Because if you love people, they will easily look past your hair being mussed or your grammatical mistakes or any other flaws you may have. But if they sense you don't love them, your every imperfection will be an irritant to them.

If you don't feel very attractive, stop focusing on your clothing or appearance for a while, and start letting your heart love people. They'll discover a new attractiveness in you!

> When you meet a man,
> you judge him by his clothes.
> When you leave a man,
> you judge him by his heart.
> *—an old Russian proverb*

Do I encourage others?

This may seem a strange question on the topic of your attractiveness, but think about someone who gives you constant, genuine encouragement. Aren't you always glad to see this person?

Being a dependable encourager is one of the best ways of being attractive to others—but what really is encouragement?

Encouragement is *bringing hope for the future.* Help people see that tomorrow can be brighter than today. Help them see that they're *becoming*—maturing and growing stronger. But a *warning* here: never give hype or false hope.

Get a clear, realistic view as you think about your friend's future. Try to imagine what his or her life will be like if improvement continues at the present rate. Reassure your friend that he or she is making great progress! Help your friend see that life will be better tomorrow than it is today. That's encouragement!

On the other hand, if you leave someone feeling that tomorrow will be worse than today, they'll naturally tend to get discouraged—and won't enjoy being around you.

When Encouragement Is Lacking

Lack of encouragement is the biggest cause of turnover in America—the big reason for kids running away, employees leaving, couples divorcing, and so on.

If you've known others who were struggling in a relationship or job, how many times have you heard them say: "He (or she) just doesn't appreciate me anymore," or "They don't seem to care whether I live or die"? What's really behind those words is this statement: "They don't *encourage* me."

Do I ask others the right questions?

Taking the time to ask people questions lets them know you *care*. Don't interrogate them, but *interview* them—discuss things with them—talk with them. Show them you care about their interests, their family, their plans and goals. Make the most of each person's uniqueness.

The right questions, asked with sincerity, can't help but make you attractive.

The Outer You

What can I learn from others who are attractive

If you can think of friends who have a look that you like, you may want to ask them where they buy their clothes or get their hair done, and so on.

Does my appearance or image match my position?

I've known many company presidents or division heads who still dress like college students. Have you experienced some progress in position that should also be reflected in your appearance and image?

A principle to remember: Like attracts like.

Do I have enough energy to be attractive?

Are you getting the rest, exercise, and right kind of food you need to keep from feeling fatigued? (See chap. 14.)

Your Image

You don't have to *create* an image. You already have one—you already have visibility. But you may need to *clarify* your image.

For example, if you've become a college professor, don't continue projecting the image of a student. If you've earned a lot of money, don't try to deceive people with a poor-as-a-church-mouse look.

As you continue clarifying and improving your image, remember to pay as much attention to internal factors as you do to the external ones.

Your Dreams

Do I have a future focus?

I've noticed that most people whose minds are focused on the past tend to be melancholy, and those who focus on the present tend to be more critical; but those who have a future focus are the most positive and attractive. Where is your focus?

A final question:

Do I really see my personal appearance as one of the best investments I can make in life?

To important people around you, your appearance makes a definite statement about who you are and what you think about yourself. What kind of statement are you making?

Several wealthy people have pointed out to me that, when it comes to image, it takes only a small investment to make a relatively big improvement in your appearance. I suggest to men that, if they have only a little money to spend on appearance, they concentrate on their hairstyle, tie, belt, and shoes. Each of these can make a major difference in a person's overall image.

Remember, too, that your appearance isn't a reflection of you alone. At different times it also reflects on your spouse, your company or organization, and others as well.

The inner you, the outer you, and your dreams—take a look at them all because others are looking too!

Remember

Remember: in the future, whenever you're feeling unattractive (or counseling someone who feels that way), pick up this book, turn to this chapter, and ask these fundamental questions:

The Inner You

- ❖ Do I have a positive attitude?
- ❖ Am I self-centered or others-centered?
- ❖ Do I really love people?
- ❖ Do I encourage others?
- ❖ Do I ask others the right questions?

The Outer You

- ❖ What can I learn from others who are attractive?
- ❖ Does my appearance or image match my position?
- ❖ Do I have enough energy to be attractive?

Your Dreams

- ❖ Do I have a future focus?
- ❖ Do I really see my personal appearance as one of the best investments I can make in life?

Knowing the right questions to ask helps increase your leadership confidence.

3 BALANCE

"Cheryl," I said to my wife in a moment I haven't forgotten, "life is a constant struggle for *balance.*"

I was about twenty-five or thirty at the time, and that single, simple statement seemed to best express my overwhelming feelings about life.

I think the statement still is true. Imbalance causes distortion and breakage in our lives—and when, after a struggle, the balance is restored, we find that it brings beauty and strength.

I'm reminded of Alexander Calder's sculptured mobiles, with their big swirling metal pieces suspended on steel wires. As long as a mobile is balanced, there is beauty. But if even one piece is yanked away, the balance and beauty are destroyed.

How in the world do you maintain personal balance at the hectic pace we live today? Everything in life seems to be going three times faster than ever before;

we have twice the responsibilities, four times the options, seventy-two times the problems, and only half the budget.

How do you maintain balance in all of that?

The blizzard feeling

I grew up in northern Michigan and can remember being outside in blizzards so blinding I couldn't see my hand in front of my face. Maybe your life sometimes seems like one of those blizzards—a lot of little pieces flying around, obscuring your vision.

A blizzard, of course, can't be a blizzard without the wind. The same is true for the blizzard feeling that overtakes our minds and our lives. By shutting off the wind, you could end the blizzard.

And you can. The wind is your *schedule.* You have to shut down your schedule to let all those pieces in your life settle to the ground, so you can see clearly.

When you feel you're in a blizzard, bring your schedule to a halt—even for as short a time as an hour. Go for a snack at a restaurant, or retreat to a park bench; go somewhere, and—to help you focus your life and regain balance—ask yourself the questions in this chapter.

Can I identify the specific areas in which I am experiencing imbalance?

I've become convinced that most people think of their lives as consisting of thousands of pieces that must constantly be kept in balance. I've seen the sense of relief expressed in their eyes when I tell them that there really are only seven categories—a much more manageable number.

I suggest that you memorize these seven categories, to help you keep them in balance. Here they are, in alphabetical order:

- family and marriage
- financial
- personal growth
- physical
- professional
- social
- spiritual

Everything you do affects the other areas. Typically, if you spend an hour exercising, you can't spend it at work. If you spend a dollar on doing something with your friends, you can't spend it on your personal growth or on your child. No matter the size of your resources, every decision you make has implications in all seven of these areas. In a sense, if you give to one, you actually are taking from the others.

That's why it's helpful to memorize the list. Then, as you approach a decision, you can always mentally review the implications for each area: "If we decide to take a week's vacation next month, what will be the financial impact, and what will be the impact on our family, on my personal growth, and on my physical, professional, social, and spiritual development?"

Suppose I've just earned an extra, unexpected thousand dollars. Should I invest it and make even more money? Should I spend it on my spouse and family (on something they've been wanting)? Or on my personal growth (perhaps an outlay for a new hobby or travel or some interesting seminars)? On my physical development (new exercise equipment or a health club membership)? On my professional development (working capital for the company)? On my social life (having parties or buying gifts for friends)? Or on my spiritual development?

By branding the list into your memory and realizing that every decision you make has implications in all seven areas, you have a constant context for making decisions and keeping in balance.

You'll also, therefore, be better able to put your finger on any specific area in which you're out of balance. Rather than having to live with a vague sense that something's wrong, you can ask, "In which of these seven areas am I actually feeling pressure?"

That's the first step toward regaining balance: pinpointing the area in which your imbalance is really happening.

With the seven basic areas of life in mind, you can go on to ask these questions:

To which of the seven areas of life have I been giving too much time, energy, and/or money?

Which area(s) have I been neglecting?

In which area(s) do I feel the most pressure, and why?

Perhaps you're feeling tremendous financial pressure, which is causing you to shift most of your mental and emotional energy in that direction. And though you may be spending time with your family, you aren't really "with" them. You're thinking about and focusing on the financial pressure you feel. In your time away from your schedule, put your finger on that point of pressure and begin asking what you can do to reduce it.

What three specific steps can I take to correct the imbalance I feel today?

If you could do just three things to cut the pressure in half—and regain 50 percent of your lost balance—what would they be? If you focus on those three areas, you can walk away from that park bench an hour later with a lot more personal balance than when you sat down.

What will be the unwanted result if I continue living with imbalance in my life?

What will go wrong? Stay in touch with reality.

Am I willing to pay the price it will take to become balanced?

Getting balanced may mean a new diet. It may mean a new exercise regimen. It may mean a new schedule. It may mean a variety of things—so are you really willing to pay the price of gaining balance? If not—are you willing to pay the price of living with imbalance?

To what (or whom) have I devoted the majority of my life energy?

If an invisible observer could somehow see and hear both your thoughts and actions, day in and day out—what would this person say you are most devoted to? Is it your family? Your career? What is the dominant preoccupation of your mind, your heart, and your life? And is that the way you want it to be?

Who or what would benefit most if my life regained a sense of balance? And who or what would lose most?

After you manage to stop the blizzard long enough to identify some critical steps to take, think about what difference taking those steps will make. Who will benefit? Who will lose? How will it affect your spouse, your children, your job, and your personal interests?

Who can help me restore my sense of life balance?

As a friend once told me, "Alone, you're always alone; but it takes only one other person to make a team." Who can you team up with in mutual accountability to regain a stronger sense of balance?

And remember that the more emotional the issue, the more deeply you need an objective outsider to help you achieve or regain balance.

A word about loneliness

Whenever you feel lonely, identify the specific kind of loneliness you feel. This is especially crucial in the process of seeking to regain balance because loneliness can be either a cause or a by-product of imbalance.

Not all loneliness is social. In fact, loneliness takes many forms:

He who knows, and knows he knows, is wise.
Follow him.
He who knows, and doesn't know he knows, is ignorant.
Enlighten him.
He who doesn't know, and doesn't know he doesn't know,
is a fool.
Avoid him.
He who doesn't know, and knows he doesn't know,
is a student.
Teach him.

- financial loneliness—when there is no one to share the financial burden
- family loneliness—when we are far from home
- physical loneliness—when there is no one to touch
- professional loneliness—when we do or see so much in our position that we cannot share
- social loneliness—when friends are absent
- spiritual loneliness—when we feel we're the only believer in the crowd

Spending time staying in balance

At first glance, a truly adequate amount of time devoted to "stopping the blizzard" will probably seem to be too much. But go ahead and count on it: commit a disproportionate amount of time keeping your life in focus and balance because both focus and balance are keys to long-term effectiveness. I need not tell you that if you don't keep in balance today, you'll suffer for it tomorrow. Life's just that way.

Remember

In the future, whenever you feel your life is getting out of control, reread this chapter. Ask yourself:

- Can I identify the specific areas in which I am experiencing imbalance?
- To which of the seven basic areas of life have I been giving too much time, energy, and/or money?
- Which area(s) have I been neglecting?
- In which area(s) do I feel the most pressure, and why?
- What three specific steps can I take to correct the imbalance I feel today?
- What will be the unwanted result if I continue living with imbalance in my life?
- Am I willing to pay the price it will take to become balanced?
- To what (or whom) have I devoted the majority of my life energy?
- Who or what would benefit most if my life regained a sense of balance? And who or what would lose most?
- Who can help me restore my sense of life balance?

Asking these questions when you're feeling imbalanced can help restore your sense of leadership confidence.

4 CHANGE

I wasn't around a century ago, but my guess is that people living back then probably felt that important changes in society—new developments that needed to be dealt with or absorbed or considered—were occurring at a rate of about once every few weeks or months. I suppose people would occasionally say, "I hear that Mr. Edison came up with a light bulb," or, "Those Wright boys are flying now—I bet we'll hear more about that."

You and I live in a different age. Significant changes seem to be happening about every nanosecond (even the words we use are changing) and happening everywhere—technological changes, political changes, social changes, economic changes—and not all of them are seen necessarily as good changes.

Change happens so fast that no one can keep up with it. It can leave you feeling overwhelmed and even depressed.

The tides of change are rolling in on a personal, individual level too, for all of us. What changes are you facing today? What changes are unsettling you? What changes do you feel you can't control?

Over the next fifty years, each time a change comes your way (such as those you face today), ask yourself these questions. I think you'll find them to be clarifying and stabilizing.

What is the context of the change?

As we've said before, nothing is meaningful without a context. How will this change affect the seven basic areas of life we discussed in the last chapter? How will it affect you professionally, spiritually, socially, financially, and so on? Make sure that you consider the impact in all seven areas, not just one. A change that may be devastating financially could be a lifesaver to your family, or to your spiritual or physical health. Always seek to understand the greater context.

> We constantly change
> the world, even by our
> inaction. Therefore, let us
> change it responsibly.
> —*Benjamin Franklin*

What things never change?

The changes you're encountering today have many implications, but certain things aren't affected in the least.

Learn to stay aware of these constants—these unchanging factors.

Some people find these constants in their spiritual faith and their life values, in their sense of calling and mission, and in the love and commitment they share with their family. Wherever you find them, don't let them go.

Changes often bring a sense of unsettledness and unreality; everything seems to be flying around. In that environment, I suggest that you follow this mental exercise: With a sheet of paper marked with the column headings shown in the example below, make a list of the things in your life that you're confident will *not* change in the next *twenty years*—for example, you'll stay married to the same spouse, you'll still have the same children, and so on. Take these, and mentally drive in a nine-inch railroad spike to hold each of them in place.

(Spike) *20 yrs.*	*(Nail)* *5 yrs.*	*(Tack)* *1 yr.*	*Other*

Then list other things that probably won't change in the next *five years*—maybe you'll still be wearing the same suit and living in the same house with the same furniture, and so on. Take two-inch nails and fasten these down as well.

Now list the things that will stay the same for the next *twelve months*—for instance, you'll probably have the same job, be driving the same car, have the same circle of friends, and so on. Use tacks to keep these in place.

So now, while everything else is still flying around, you've nailed down probably 80 percent of your life—the things that are relatively stable. Being aware of that stability can help you keep your equilibrium.

We can also develop an appreciation for things that change very slowly. I grew up in Mancelona, Michigan, and it changes—but not very often, and not very fast.

What are the logical versus the psychological aspects of this change?

A change can make sense logically, but can still lead to anxiety in the psychological dimension. Everyone needs a niche, and when the niche starts to change after we've become comfortable in it, it causes stress and insecurities. So before introducing change, we have to consider the psychological dimension.

A good exercise when you face change is to make a list of the logical advantages and disadvantages that should result from the change and then another list indicating the psychological impact. Just seeing this on a sheet of paper can be clarifying. You may find yourself saying, "I don't like to admit it, but I'm insecure on this point, even though the change makes sense logically."

Another possibility is that a change you're considering may not affect your psychological security, yet it doesn't make sense logically when you examine the advantages and disadvantages.

The key is to distinguish between the logical and the psychological aspects of any change.

> Taking a new step, uttering a new word,
> is what people fear most.
> —*Dostoevski*

Remember, too, that as a leader, you must know how to deal with more than just the ways changes affect you. You must also be keenly aware of how the changes you decide on and implement will impact the lives of others. Seemingly simple decisions you make may profoundly impact other people's livelihood, or their social or professional confidence, or a host of other areas. You want to be supersensitive to the full implications of changes you initiate.

When you're announcing a change to those affected by it, don't just say, "This makes sense, doesn't it, staff?" Before you announce the change, anticipate their psychological reactions.

Even the most positive of changes can tend to make *someone* look like or feel that he or she has failed. So you can expect resistance and defensiveness.

The Essence

When it comes to things you need to know for dealing effectively with change, here's the essence:

Change represents both possible opportunity and potential loss.

It's helpful to remember that change can be seen as either *revolutionary* (something totally different from what has been) or *evolutionary* (a refinement of what has been). You'll usually find it easier to present change as a simple refinement of "the way we've been doing it" rather than something big and new and different.

> One key to all planning is the word *evolution.*
> You start in a direction,
> and your plans keep evolving.
> —*Gary Weaver*

What are the advantages of the change?

You may also want to list the *three main advantages* you see in this change, especially if the change is imposed from the outside. It's likely that those advantages are real, though you may have been so caught up in thinking about the disadvantages that you haven't looked carefully at the positive side. And when you need to announce a change to your staff, you may want to stress the three main advantages that the change will bring.

Am I changing too much too fast?

Should you allow this change? If something is changing when it shouldn't, it's better to oppose that change from the beginning than to wait until it has taken deeper root.

Finally, ask yourself these questions:

Is this change temporary or permanent?

Is my attitude toward change right? Do I have the right appreciation for it?

What negative aspects of this change need creative problem solving?

WHAT TO CHANGE—AND WHAT NOT TO

It is IBM's credo that any organization, in order to survive and to achieve success, must have a sound set of beliefs on which it bases all its policies and actions.

But more important than having a set of beliefs is faithful adherence to those beliefs. If any organization is to meet the challenges of a changing world, it must be prepared to change everything about itself except those beliefs, as it moves through its present to its future.

Let me reiterate. The basic philosophy, the very spirit and drive of an organization, has far more to do with its relative achievements than do technical or economic resources, organizational structure, innovation, and timing.

—*T. J. Watson Jr.*
(former IBM board chairman)

Remember

When you face changes in the future, these questions can help you keep perspective:

- What is the context of the change?
- What things never change?
- What are the logical versus the psychological aspects of this change?
- What are the advantages of the change?
- Am I changing too much too fast? Should I allow this change?
- Is this change temporary or permanent?
- Is my attitude toward change right? Do I have the right appreciation for it?
- What negative aspects of this change need creative problem solving?

Asking the right questions can give you focus amid a storm of change, and so increase your leadership confidence.

5 COMMUNICATION

What message do you most want to communicate convincingly to someone in the next thirty days?

It may be persuading customers to buy your product or service, or finding a buyer for your used car, or motivating someone to marry you, or inspiring someone to work harder or to do better on school grades. Whatever it is, focus it clearly in mind as you read this chapter.

As you try to convey this message, the most important principle to remember is the one expressed in the Golden Rule from the Bible: "Just as you want others to treat you, treat them in the same way." It's just as much a golden rule for conveying messages as it is for conduct. In fact, the Golden Essence of Communicating could be stated: *Just as you want people to communicate with you, communicate with them in the same way.* It's the most profound principle of communication.

Let's look at questions that can help you communicate effectively.

Who is my audience?

First, get a clear picture of who you're trying to convince. If it's only one person, that's relatively easy. But if it's a group of people, this focusing will take effort. You must ask, "Who are they as individuals? What are the common denominators among them? What do they need? What do they want? What are their struggles? What will they respond to? What will they resist?"

Put yourself in your listeners' shoes. That's the key to getting your message across, no matter what medium you choose.

The following questions can help you better focus on and comprehend your audience.

If I were to write a speech that captured fully the way my audience will most likely respond to what I'm communicating, what would the speech say?

Put your audience's perspective into words. Remember that the people you're addressing have certain assumptions and conclusions and values that they hang onto. How will these influence their responses?

Dr. Jerry Ballard, former president of World Relief, says that "all miscommunications are the result of differing assumptions." When I first heard that from Jerry, I thought his statement was too bold and broad. For three years I tried to find an exception to it, but couldn't. Ever since then I've been *teaching* it! Jerry's observation explains why there can be so much frustration and pressure even when people are trying to communicate—it's because the speaker is assuming one thing and the listener another.

What assumptions are shared by your audience but not by you? And what assumptions are *you* making that they aren't?

What will most strongly influence my audience to accept my communication?

What will most strongly influence them to reject my communication?

What will be their three major reasons for wanting to do what you want them to do, and what will be their three major reasons for *not* wanting to do it? Also determine which of these reasons is most important.

What are my audience's five most predictable points of resistance?

What will be their three most likely misconceptions about my idea?

This question focuses not on areas where your audience will disagree with you, but on where they're most likely to simply misunderstand.

The tone of your communication will play a big role in how it's understood. Lord Chesterfield wrote, "Ninety percent of all friction in daily life is caused by mere tone of voice. When a man speaks, his words convey his thoughts, and his tone his mood."

What you say may not be as important as how it is said. Consider the difference between two examples that Donna Kelly gives: the husband who tells his wife, "Darling, when I look at you, time stands still"; and the one who says, "Darling, you have a face that would stop a clock."

What are the facts involved? And what are the benefits related to each of those facts?

What are the three or four facts you're trying to communicate? Do you know the facts well, through your own experience? If you must constantly quote "authorities" and "experts," then you will not be seen as an expert yourself.

And of course, you want to present more than just the facts—you also want to convey the benefits associated with each one.

One of my clients recently was considering whether to hire a person for a senior staff position. The man had already been with the organization for a few months on a trial basis. Here's how their "Facts/Benefits" list looked:

FACTS

1. Paul has received the unanimous approval of our entire leadership team.
2. Paul has been with us in a leadership position for fifteen weeks, and feedback about him is positive.
3. Paul is 45.

BENEFITS

1. If we hire him, we'll feel good about the fact that there was no hesitation in our minds concerning him. We'll have a real sense that he's been part of the team from the beginning.
2. We've observed him in action, so we all feel well acquainted with him.
3. He's old enough to have maturity and experience, yet young enough to grow with us.

With this clear thinking, the organization's leaders can make and communicate with confidence the decision to hire Paul.

Why does my audience need to hear this message?

Would I agree with the idea if someone else tried to communicate it to me? Why or why not?

Would you buy it from someone else? If not, don't try to sell it.

Am I making the message irresistible? What are the value and price considerations?

Every choice we make is the result of a process in which we weigh the *price* of that choice against the *value* that we perceive it brings.

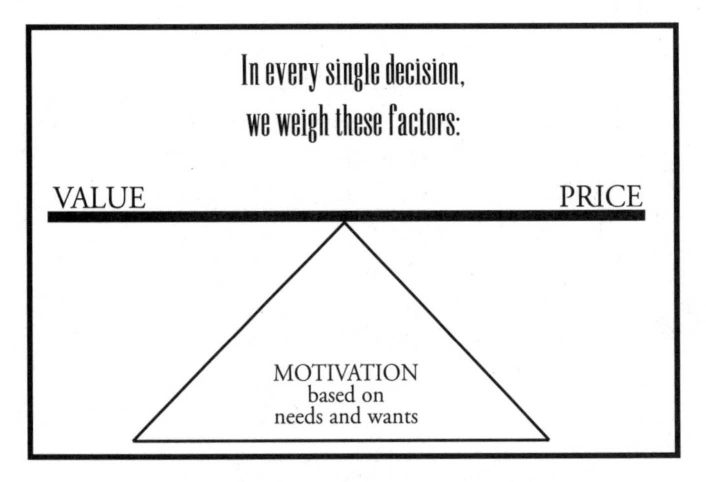

Let's say, for example, you go into a store and see a watch you like, and the sales clerk tells you, "It's a hundred dollars."

You look at it closely and say to yourself, "I've shopped around, and it's worth a hundred dollars." Then you think, *Based on my need and desire for a watch, am I motivated today to spend the hundred dollars for which I've had to work hard to earn? Or is that price too high?*

The more money you make and have, the less critical the price seems. If you make five dollars an hour, one hundred dollars for a watch is a big price to pay; if you make a hundred dollars an hour, it isn't that much. But if you have the money, and if the perceived value of the watch is higher than or equal to the price, you'll buy the watch. If the value you perceive is lower than the price, you won't.

While you're thinking this over, the sales clerk says to you, "We want you to have the watch; for the next five minutes only, we'll lower the price to ten dollars."

Suddenly you're more than eager to close the deal. You know you can get something of relatively high value for a relatively low price—which is what makes something *irresistible.* Everyone likes a bargain.

Now come back to the message you want to communicate to someone in the next thirty days. What will be the perceived value of the idea you want your audience to accept? And what price are you asking your audience to pay? When you compare those two, are you giving your audience an irresistible bargain? If not, how can you either reduce the price you're asking or increase the value—or, best of all, do both?

Make your message irresistible. Until it is, it isn't ready.

How can I visualize—tangibly, or with word pictures—the rightness, the value, and the uniqueness of my message?

Think through how to visualize your message with illustrations, demonstrations, cartoons, charts, diagrams, or other visual aids. Remember, a picture is worth a thousand words, and a good graph or chart is worth ten thousand numbers.

A final thought: As you convey your message, *focus on communication, not content.* Your content should be so familiar to you that you can forget it and instead give your utmost attention to truly *connecting* and *communicating* with your audience.

Remember

In the future, when you're trying to communicate a specific message of any kind, these questions can help you achieve crystal-clear communication:

- ❖ Who is my audience?
- ❖ If I were to write a speech that captured fully the way my audience will most likely respond to what I'm communicating, what would the speech say?
- ❖ What will most strongly influence my audience to accept my communication?
- ❖ What will most strongly influence them to reject my communication?
- ❖ What are my audience's five most predictable points of resistance?
- ❖ What will be their three most likely misconceptions about my idea?
- ❖ What are the facts involved? And what are the benefits related to each of those facts?
- ❖ Why does my audience need to hear this message?
- ❖ Would I agree with the idea if someone else tried to communicate it to me? Why or why not?
- ❖ Am I making the message irresistible? What are the value and price considerations?
- ❖ How can I visualize—tangibly, or with word pictures—the rightness, the value, and the uniqueness of my message?

Ask these questions to clarify your communications and keep increasing your leadership confidence.

6 CONFIDENCE

It might surprise you to learn that of the hundreds of executives I've worked with over the past several years, probably half of them—in the privacy of their car, in a consulting session, or in a personal conversation—have questioned their own competence, asking whether they're really right for the job. They were struggling with a lack of confidence to succeed or to carry out their dream; they wondered if they were kidding themselves about being the right person for their job.

Their insecurities aren't unusual. It may seem to you that true leaders never doubt themselves or their own ability, but I believe 90 percent of them face these doubts at one time or another.

And yet to lead others confidently, you must have a certain faith in yourself. You must trust your motives and your recommendations. Unless you believe in your own presentation, your own program, your own dreams, others will not feel confident to follow you.

You may be struggling to gain confidence today, and if not today, you're likely to be at some point in the next three years.

The following questions and principles can help guide you through those moments of self-doubt.

In the situation that gives me anxiety and a lack of confidence, am I being too self-centered?

Frankly, I've learned that the anxiety associated with a lack of confidence is frequently a symptom of self-centeredness. If you're self-centered today, you're probably anxious—and the reverse is also true. At the bottom line, anxiety is self-centeredness.

Think right now about some situation in which you want more confidence. In that situation, are you considering the needs and interests of others? Or are you focusing almost exclusively on yourself and your concerns about not coming across as unwise or weak or indecisive? Is your desire to be *giving* to others in this situation, or is it to be *getting* something from them? Are you afraid that others will not give you the attention and recognition and affirmation you need? Or are you thinking about how you can provide what *they* need to succeed?

Perhaps you're worried about a special presentation or speech you have to make. Clients often tell me that in the normal operation of their business they have all the confidence in the world, but when they're asked to speak at a seminar or some other big gathering, their anxiety is overwhelming.

I tell them, "Look, when you get up on the platform, just forget yourself. A year from now most of them won't recall your name or what you said, and five years from now they'll probably have no remembrance of you even speaking to them. After all, how many speakers do you think you've listened to in your life? And how many of them can you remember, not only who they were, but also the points they made?

"I'm not belittling what you've got to tell them," I say, "or the impact you can have. But don't get too caught up in your own importance, and especially in how you look. It will take them only a week to forget what color suit you were wearing.

Before you leave home, make sure your hair is combed and your suit is neat—that kind of thing—but then ignore yourself, and start focusing totally on the people you'll be speaking to: Who are they? What are their real needs? What can I say to help meet those needs?

> The opposite of loving others is not hating them, but rather being self-centered.

When I'm on a platform and about to speak, if I feel anxious, I start looking at the people in the audience individually. I look at a face in the front row, and in my mind I say to that person, *I don't know you, but I care about you, and I want to see you win. I know you probably have personal needs in the area we're looking at today, and I have good news for you. If you'll listen to the principles I discuss and apply them to your life, you really will be helped.*

Then I focus my eyes on the next person, and say the same thing, and then the next, and so on.

By the time I reach the faces on the second or third row, my anxiety has gone away. It's been replaced by an enthusiasm for telling people something that I know will help them.

What realistically is the worst thing that could happen in this situation?

You'll gain confidence as you understand that even if the worst happens, you'll still make it.

Who can I call for help in this situation?

Who are your friends and acquaintances, your network of people who can shore you up in an area in which you may not be personally accomplished?

> The more you really know, the more confident you become to admit what you don't know.

I recommend that you keep a "Lifelong Friends List," and continually add to it. Include not only people close by but also people you know who may now live halfway around the world and yet, if you were able to again spend time with them, you know your friendship would deepen.

Who are the friends who will love me regardless of whether I win or lose in this situation and in life?

These are people who support you and enjoy being with you no matter what happens. Your confidence will grow as you think about their commitment to you, as you realize you don't have to win at everything to be accepted and loved by them.

In what area do I have a feeling of expertise?

I often meet people who say—usually with a little embarrassment—"I'm a jack of all trades and master of none." If you put yourself in that category, I urge you to start mastering something—to understand some area as completely as you can. It could be auto mechanics or running a farm or teaching a class on a certain subject. Whatever it is, by mastering it you'll gain an internal confidence that is unknown to those with a jack-of-all-trades approach to life.

What are my primary strengths, gifts, and talents?

Another way of discovering these is to ask, "What have I done well in the past?"

To help you be alert to these, I suggest that you maintain a "Positive Progress List," as described in the box on the next page.

Your Positive Progress List

Set aside time now to list all the positive milestones you have reached in your life. Whenever you're tempted to be discouraged, review this list. It can be an emotional lifesaver, bringing you back to the surface when a wave of doubt or despair washes over you.

What is my greatest strength?

Peter Drucker tells leaders, "Identify your greatest single strength, *and maximize it.*" Not four or five strengths, but the greatest *one.*

What am I doing when I feel best about myself?

Can I enlarge my involvement in this activity? If so, how?

In what area of life do I have a natural interest in growing personally?

When you're growing personally, you tend to gain confidence. When you're stagnating, you tend to lose it.

What's the focus of my life?

Use the Life Focus Chart (see chap. 16) to help you focus on what you truly want to do and be in the future. When you know where you're going and what you're becoming long-term, it helps you remain confident while going through today's anxiety and turbulence.

Remember

Whenever you're anxious about your future or you question your abilities, ask yourself these questions:

- In the situation that gives me anxiety and a lack of confidence, am I being too self-centered?
- What realistically is the worst thing that could happen in this situation?
- Who can I call for help in this situation?
- Who are the friends who will love me regardless of whether I win or lose in this situation and in life?
- In what area do I have a feeling of expertise?
- What are my primary strengths, gifts, and talents?
- What is my greatest strength?
- What am I doing when I feel best about myself?
- In what area of life do I have a natural interest in growing personally?
- What's the focus of my life?

Knowing and asking the right questions will increase your leadership confidence.

7 CREATIVITY

On a one-to-ten scale, how would you respond to these questions?

- How creative do you feel you are?
- How creative would you like to be?

How much distance is there between your two numbers?

Before you put the one-to-ten scales away, let me ask two more questions:

- How competent are you at solving problems?
- How artistic are you?

I believe that creativity for leaders is, in essence, bringing together new and workable solutions to whatever problems they face. *Creativity for leaders finds its true expression in problem solving.*

Therefore I would say you really are creative if, in your answers to the questions above, you gave yourself a fairly high mark for problem solving—even if you don't rate yourself as highly artistic.

We commonly equate artistic ability with creativity, but that's a mistake. In fact, rather than *creating*, many artists are only *duplicating* something—in a drawing or painting, for example—though they do it very skillfully.

It's a fundamental misconception to think, "To be creative, I have to be artistic." If you can solve a problem in personnel relations or in sales or production or on the computer or at the planning table, then you're creative.

Before going on, I'd like to ask you to focus on the one thing you currently have the strongest desire to create. Maybe it's a new concept in salt shakers, or a new automobile. Perhaps it's a new building design, a new sales program, or an article of clothing you want to design and sew. Whatever it is, it's something that you want to make in a new and different way so that people can look at it and say, "How creative!"

Asking yourself the following questions can help enhance your ability to be creative:

Do I have an attitude of readiness for creativity?

In your area of focus, do you believe the best ideas have already been developed? Or do you believe they're yet to come?

I'm told that the director of the U.S. Patent Office in the late 1800s wanted to close that agency because he believed all the best ideas had already been patented. Is that your mind-set as well? Do you believe the best has already been, or are you convinced the best is yet to be?

> I have no special gift—I am only
> passionately curious.
> —*Albert Einstein*

In the area in which I want to apply creativity, what is the need or problem?

As you think about the creative task you've identified, how can you restate it as a *need* or *problem*—and then simply solve it using the problem-solving skills you possess? *Need* is the mother of creativity.

How can you state *your* need for creativity as a problem, and then simply solve the problem?

> Limitations are absolutely essential to creativity.
> In an interaction with limits,
> the creative act comes into being.
> —*Rollo May, The Courage to Change*

I've published a book called *The Memories Book,* and many people have told me how creative an idea it is. It's a gift book that includes six hundred questions with blank lines for parents or grandparents to record their memories about various aspects of their lives. It lets them leave a priceless written legacy for their children and their children's children.

However, *The Memories Book* started out simply as an attempt to meet the needs of my wife's elderly grandmother, Frances Shupe, who had a lot of lonely hours in the evenings or in the middle of the night when she couldn't sleep. I saw the problem and worked to solve it; the solution was an appealing concept that could be passed on to others.

When a need or problem is burning a hole in your mind and you think, "There's got to be a solution to this," recognize that need or problem as the right soil for creativity. Stay in pursuit. Reflect deeply on the need or problem, and the right solution will jump out at you.

Should I start from scratch to find an original solution for this need? Or is there a model or example I can follow?

There are at least two distinct types of human creativity. Both are equally valuable and acceptable, and they can also be equally effective.

- *Original creativity* is the process whereby you arrive at a solution without having seen anything like it previously. The solution is simply one that makes sense to you, so you use it. A person who is originally creative usually prefers (and even insists on) being given a "blank sheet of paper" for solving a problem. This person finds fulfillment in seeing and building the solution himself. Ideas that have been seen or tried before are almost automatically tossed out for not being "fresh." He feels that someone else's pattern just gets in the way, and wants to know, "How can I do this in an original way?"

- *Adaptive creativity* is the process in which you take an existing model or approach—or maybe two or three—and tailor it to fit your situation. You learn from others, and you make their ideas work for you. When solving a problem, a person with adaptive creativity usually prefers (and strongly relies on) previous solutions to similar problems. His attitude is, "Why reinvent the wheel?"

Understand which of these approaches you prefer, and which one is preferred by the people you work with, then take advantage of it.

How can I expand my perspective?

Look back at the Mind-Stretcher Questions in chapter 1. By temporarily adjusting the context within which you approach the problem, these questions often lead you to see new options, new possibilities, and new solutions.

For example, perhaps you're trying to solve a problem on which you can spend a hundred dollars. One of the Mind-Stretcher Questions is, "What changes would I make if I had an unlimited budget?" With a thousand or a million dollars available, you could identify a variety of totally different solutions that you never considered before. And you start to see ways in which some of them could be pursued on a scaled-down, hundred-dollar version. You return to reality, but with an expanded perspective that sees new possibilities.

Another idea for expanding your view: Take sixty seconds (or maybe five minutes) to list as many options as you can. Don't worry now about the drawbacks to any of them. Just go for quantity. You may be surprised by your own creative solutions.

> When something is simple—
> keep simplifying it!

Make sure you have plenty of big sheets of paper to write on, not only for this exercise, but for all your creative thinking and brainstorming. Big problems need big pieces of paper.

Is this need or problem really worth a lot of time?

Make sure the problem—and the creative solution you're seeking—are worth the amount of time and mental energy you're exerting. Sometimes they aren't.

How do I feel about the problem or need?

Often, simply realizing how you *feel* about a need or solution will prompt different creative approaches to a solution.

Has someone already solved this problem?

There's no need to reinvent the wheel. (On the other hand, never stop refining the tire!)

Who else could help me creatively think through this problem?

Who's the most creative person you have easy access to? When you're stuck on a problem, give that person a quick call (perhaps only five minutes), clearly explain the problem, and ask for some creative input. Expect to hear some creative alternatives!

Could this solution be a really "Big Winner"?

Some creative solutions can be thought of as ten-dollar ideas, while others might be million-dollar ideas. Don't spend too much time and energy on the ten-dollar ideas. Instead, identify the big ones, and invest yourself there.

Finally, always remember: *You're far more creative than you think you are.*

The Joy—and the Journey—of Creativity

In the light of knowledge attained, the happy achievement seems almost a matter of course, and any intelligent student can grasp it without too much trouble. But the years of anxious searching in the dark, with their intense longing, their alternations of confidence and exhaustion, and the final emergence into light—only those who have themselves experienced it can understand that.

—*Albert Einstein*

Remember

Whenever you're tempted to doubt your creative abilities, ask yourself these key questions:

- Do I have an attitude of readiness for creativity?
- In the area in which I want to apply creativity, what is the need or problem?
- Should I start from scratch to find an original solution for this need? Or is there a model or example I can follow?
- How can I expand my perspective?
- Is this need or problem really worth a lot of time?
- How do I feel about the problem or need?
- Has someone already solved this problem?
- Who else could help me creatively think through this problem?
- Could this solution be a really "Big Winner"?

By knowing the right questions, you'll continue to increase your leadership confidence.

8 DECISION MAKING

Most leaders must constantly work at *making decisions simple.* The implications of a decision will always be complex enough, and sometimes we try to solve or deal with all the implications—the how, who, why, how much, and so on—at the same time we make the decision.

These implications, of course, must be considered, but first you should simply clarify the *what:* In its simplest form, *what is the decision I am trying to make? What are the options?* Once you've singled out the decision's essence, you can look at the implications in the right perspective.

Before we continue, ask yourself: *What's the most important decision I need to make today?* Perhaps you're facing a decision like one of these: Should we go on vacation? Should I get married? Should I change jobs? Should we pursue this new account? Should we hire this person, or fire that person?

Whatever it is, keep that approaching decision in mind as we go through the following questions and explore new perspectives on the decision-making process. (If the decision involves major risk, you'll find chap. 29 on "Risk Taking" to be helpful as well.)

What are the five to ten most relevant, proven facts in this situation? And what are the fundamental assumptions I'm making about this situation?

Right up front, distinguish proven *facts* from what are simply your assumptions. Assumptions are what we believe to be true, but have not proven. They can be very faulty foundations on which to build your decision. A proven fact is: "Last month the house across the street sold for *X* dollars." An assumption is: "I think houses in this neighborhood will generally sell for about *X* dollars."

In my work with executives, I've found that the most frequent violation of sound decision-making principles is trying to decide before all the facts are known. Somehow in our minds we have a need to decide *now,* a need to bring closure, a need to have things settled. Because an undecided situation often brings us stress, our minds compel us to make a decision too quickly before the facts are in. We decide on the basis of three facts and seventeen hunches, rather than seventeen facts and three hunches.

Hundreds of times a year I find good occasion to quote Peter Drucker's words, "Once the facts are clear, the decisions jump out at you." So find the facts.

Decision making ... or Escape?

Speed in making up one's mind is not an important element in successful choices. In fact, the snap decision is often not a decision at all, but a technique of avoidance. Though it created an illusion of command, a lightning choice may mean only that someone has snatched at the handiest alternative rather than come to grips with the real issues involved.

—*Dr. Joyce Brothers*

How will this decision impact all the people involved?

Who are the main players? And who else will be affected? People in other departments? Your spouse and children?

What will be the long-term impact of this decision?

How will this decision affect people a year from now? Five years or ten years from now? By the time the children leave home? By the time I retire?

The more reversible the decision and its consequences, the freer you are to move faster in making it.

> Be careful the environment you choose . . .
> For it will shape you.
> Be careful the friends you choose . . .
> For you will become like them.
> —*W. Clement Stone*

What legal, moral, or ethical concerns are involved in this decision?

Be clear on these factors, especially if it's a big decision involving major commitments of money, time, and energy, and affecting a number of lives.

Understand the difference between these three categories. In my working definitions, *legality* is based on coded law, *morality* on a moral code or truth, and *ethics* on accepted local or cultural standards—such as common business standards. Something is *illegal* if it violates the law. Something is *immoral* if it violates a moral standard or truth. Something is *unethical* if it doesn't conform to a standard, acceptable practice.

Sort out these terms and their application to your decision-making process, since some decisions you make could be legal and yet immoral, or ethical and yet illegal.

Have I written down the basic issues involved in this decision?

Simply getting everything on paper can be very helpful—and the bigger the decision, the more helpful it is.

What Mind-Stretcher Questions should I ask about this decision?

Again, look back at the Mind-Stretcher Questions in chapter 1.

What are the trends related to this decision?

As stated before, *nothing is meaningful without a context.* A trend line is one way to help you establish a context for sound decision making. As trends change, the context changes, and therefore the meaning of each fact you're considering also changes. What are the trends related to the major decision you're making? Are prices going up or down? Is demand greater or less? Are complaints fewer or more frequent?

What other lingering questions do I have?

Maybe you've been ignoring some of the questions or concerns in your mind. Bring them out into the open and be sure you deal with them before you make the decision.

Finally, for an even fuller perspective, I encourage you to use the list of additional questions on the following pages whenever you face a major decision.

25 Questions to Ask before Making Major Decisions

Note: Not every question in this list will help you in every situation. This is simply a checklist to help you keep from overlooking important considerations before confirming and carrying out major decisions.

These questions are to be asked in addition to the other questions presented in this chapter.

1. At its essence—in one sentence—What is the decision I'm really facing? What is the "bottom, bottom line"?
2. Am I dealing with a cause or a symptom? A means or an end?
3. Am I thinking about this situation with a clear head, or am I fatigued to the point that I shouldn't be making major decisions?
4. What would the ideal solution be in this situation?
5. Should I seek outside counsel in making this decision?
6. What are the hidden agendas that are "pushing" for a decision in this situation? Why do "we" or "they" want a change? What is the source of the emotional fuel that is driving this decision?
7. If I had to decide in the next two minutes, what decision would I make, and why?
8. What decision would I expect each of my three most respected advisers to favor in this situation?
9. Can an overall decision in this situation be divided into parts, with "subdecisions" made at a few "go/no go" points along the way?
10. What are the key assumptions in my thinking that underlie the decision I'm leaning toward? What do I assume it will cost? What do I assume will be its real benefits?

11. Who? What? When? Where? Why? How? How much?
12. Have I given myself twenty-four hours to let this decision settle in my mind?
13. Is this decision consistent with our values in the past, or does it mark a change in direction or standards?
14. How will this decision affect our overall master plan? Will it sidetrack us?
15. Will this decision help to maximize my (and our) key strengths?
16. Have I verified what the results have been for others who have made a similar decision in similar circumstances? Have I checked this thoroughly?
17. How do I really feel about this decision?
18. Is this the decision I would make if our budget was twice as large as it is? Half as large? Five times as large? One-tenth as large? Is it the same decision I would make if we had twice as many staff members? Half as many?
19. What would happen if we did not carry out this decision?
20. If we didn't carry it out, what would be the best three alternative decisions?
21. Is this the best timing for carrying out this decision? If not now, why? And when?
22. Is this decision truly appropriate in scope and size to the situation we face? Am I possibly hunting an elephant with a BB gun, or a rabbit with a cannon?
23. How does my family feel about this decision? How will it affect them?
24. What aspects of the problem will not be resolved or solved by this decision?
25. Should we write a policy about this decision to guide us in similar situations in the future?

Remember

Whenever you face a big decision in the future, turn to this chapter, and ask yourself these important questions:

- What are the five to ten most relevant, proven facts in this situation? And what are the fundamental assumptions I'm making about this situation?
- How will this decision impact all the people involved?
- What will be the long-term impact of this decision?
- What legal, moral, or ethical concerns are involved in this decision?
- Have I written down the basic issues involved in this decision?
- What Mind-Stretcher Questions should I ask about this decision?
- What are the trends related to this decision?
- What other lingering questions do I have?

When it's time for decisiveness, simply asking the right questions helps increase your leadership confidence.

9 DELEGATING

I recently spent two days with the senior executive of a fast-growing organization. He was on the borderline of major burnout. Why? Because as his organization grew over the past few years, he took on more and more responsibilities himself without effectively delegating them to other people.

When I see leaders suffering burnout, I first ask, "Do they have the ability to build a staff?" and "Do they have the right people around them to effectively share the load?" How would you answer those questions about yourself?

Here's a belief of mine that frequently surprises people: *In determining your leadership competence, your ability to delegate effectively is far more important than your innate intelligence.*

Do you agree?

A person may be brilliant, yet his only contribution is what he himself can do. Someone else may be less gifted, but he or she knows how to mobilize others and, therefore, gets ten or fifteen times as much accomplished as a brighter person working alone.

It's like the difference between an outstanding quarterback who tries to play the game by himself, and one who may be less talented but who knows how to make the best use of the ends, the backs, and his offensive line. Only the second quarterback has a chance to win the game.

> If you're doing something that someone else could do at least 80 percent as well as you could, then you're more than likely wasting time.

Every leader is wise to ask constantly, "How can I appropriately bring my staff's strength to bear in this situation?" Mark Twain said it humorously: "Never learn to do anything. Then you'll always find someone else to do it for you."

Take a look at your "to do" list today. What items on this list could someone else do at least 80 percent as well as you could? Which of these would you most like to delegate today?

Exactly *what* needs to be done?

This question sounds too simple to be valuable, but it isn't. Define with crystal clarity exactly what you want accomplished before you ask someone else to do it.

Why does it need to be done?

As you delegate a task, you should also explain *why* the task needs to be done.

You may think, "Well, Bobb, I don't usually tell people *why* I want them to do something; I just tell them to do it, and I expect them to get it done!" Of course, you *are* the boss, and you don't have to tell others your reasons for wanting something done, but that approach is likely to cost you time in the long run. If you ask someone to buy something for you, and it isn't available, he can always look for a suitable (or even better) replacement if he knows *why* you wanted it in the first place. Otherwise he can only return and say, "It can't be found."

When does it need to be done?

When will the task end? People like a sense of completion, of closure. Some like it more than others and need to see measurable progress every day, while others can live with more open-endedness. Still everyone ultimately wants a conclusion, allowing him to go on to what's next. So as you delegate a task, define its end point or deadline.

Who is the best person to do it?

Obviously, until you have answers to the above questions, you can't easily select the best person for the task.

How well must it be done?

How thorough must the job be done? Do you want ten minutes of work, or ten hours, or ten days?

How much budget is available for getting it done?

As you assign responsibility, make sure you also assign the financial resources needed to carry it out. If no money is available, and the person given the task assumes expenses will be covered, you can be in trouble fast.

What training is needed for doing this task?

Make sure the person given the job will feel comfortable in it.

As you assign responsibilities to your staff, you may want to use a color code to quickly gauge each person's sense of readiness for the task. Ask her: "How do you feel about this assignment? Are you red, yellow, or green?"

Green means "I feel comfortable with it. I've done it before. There should be no problem. You can trust me."

Yellow means "I feel a little anxious, but I think I can pull it off. If I run into any trouble, I'll get back to you."

Red means "I've never done it before; I'm overwhelmed at the thought of it, and I don't know where to start."

When you get a red answer, you may need to provide training, perhaps by first doing the task yourself as a model.

What reports do I need from the person who does it?

When the job is completed, how much do you want to know about it? Do you want a complete written report? (See chap. 28 on "Reporting.")

Who else may need to be aware of this assignment?

The person you assign the project to may need to work with a team of people. If so, make sure the team is aware of the assignment.

If it isn't done, what difference will it make?

Maybe this task is something that should be left on the back burner for now. If it's not the right time for *you* to do it, it may not be the right time for your staff to do it either.

What's Your Leadership Style?

The *professional-style* leader assumes that he himself is most frequently the appropriate resource; the *executive-style* leader assumes that it's his role to find the person who's the right resource.

The *professional-style* leader frequently likes to prepare draft one himself, and let someone else review or refine it; the *executive-style* leader frequently likes to have someone else do the first draft, and then review and refine it himself.

What's *your* leadership style? Study your own patterns to find out and to avoid feeling frustrated with others whose style is different from your own.

Remember

When you want to bring the resources of others to bear on the responsibilities that weigh you down, turn to this chapter and ask yourself these questions:

- Exactly *what* needs to be done?
- *Why* does it need to be done?
- *When* does it need to be done?
- *Who* is the best person to do it?
- *How well* must it be done?
- How much budget is available for getting it done?
- What training is needed for doing the task?
- What reports do I need from the person who does it?
- Who else may need to be aware of this assignment?
- If it isn't done, what difference will it make?

Asking the right questions will help increase your leadership confidence.

10 DEPRESSION

Everyone gets depressed occasionally—hopeless, helpless, sad. But depression makes it extremely difficult to lead. The faster you can get out of it, the better.

"So what's new, Bobb?" you may say. That statement is obviously true, but it's also *profoundly* true. When depression hits, you need to get out, and fast.

> Occasional depression is humanly unavoidable; consistent depression is dangerous.

But how? What's the key to climbing out?

Today you may be on top of the world. But I encourage you to absorb this chapter's content and keep it as an ace-in-the-hole for the day—six months or two years from now—when you are staring at depression face to face. Also, store up these principles as a resource for sharing with a friend who is depressed.

Whenever you encounter depression, ask yourself these questions:

Why am I depressed?

This may seem too obvious a question, so let me rephrase it: What *benefit* am I getting from this depression?

Does that question surprise you? Instead of candidly telling someone, “Look, I need to be appreciated today. I need to be reassured,” are you hoping someone will notice your depression and pay more attention to you? If so, you probably aren't fooling anyone. Be honest with yourself.

What specific things are weighing heavily on me today?

Make a list, and make sure to write down everything!

Am I angry at anyone?

Are you really upset with someone? Do you want to tell someone off, or “punch out his lights?”

Maybe you're unable to express that anger, and so you're mentally beating up yourself for not being able to beat up someone else. Depression can ensue.

So find out who you're angry at today. Write down the person's name. Do your best to forgive that person for whatever he's done to offend you. That forgiveness is absolutely the greatest cure for anger-caused depression.

Am I physically or mentally fatigued?

Fatigue often brings on a feeling of hopelessness and helplessness. Look at chapter 14 ("Fatigue") for help with this subject. "When depressed—get rest!"

Have I been experiencing too much change too fast?

My experience is that depression often results from the disorientation we experience when we're in the middle of constant, hard-driving change. The questions in chapter 4 ("Change") can help you here.

Am I seeing my situation with a long-term perspective?

Hope returns when we look at our situation from a long-term perspective. We do not have to depend on our own present strength. As Cervantes said centuries ago, "Man's extremity is God's opportunity."

Do I have clear and meaningful goals for the future?

The kind of clear and meaningful goals that dispel depression may be as simple as deciding to read a book by next week—some decisive action that gets you beyond feeling that things will never change or improve.

Setting meaningful longer-range goals is also important in helping you reach conclusions such as, "I don't have the money I need now, but a year from now I will."

What milestones in my past can cheer me up at this time?

Again, a Positive Progress List (see chap. 6) can help you here. If you don't have such a list, sit down now and create one. What are all the things you've done right?

A friend in the midst of depression once called me. After he talked for a while, I said, "Look, you've done so many things right." "Name *one*," he said.

I asked him to get a pencil and paper, and in the next ten minutes—ten minutes that transformed the emotional tone of his spirit—we were able to list forty-three things he had done right. He recognized that his life hadn't been such a tremendous waste after all, and he knew he would have more successes in the future.

I often have that experience myself. When I'm discouraged, my wife, Cheryl, suggests that I look at my Positive Progress List. As I do, I gain perspective and hope for the future. Things have gone right in the past, and things will go right in the future. There *is* hope.

What friend can I call to cheer me up at this time?

There's nothing wrong with occasionally calling a good friend and saying, "Hey, I'm down. I need some encouragement."

What positive, specific step can I take right now—no matter how small?

The feeling of helplessness often results from having so much to do that you feel you can't possibly complete it all.

When you feel that way, list on paper the fifty or seventy or however many things you have to do. "All right," you can say, "it's impossible to get it all done this week, but what one or two specific things can I accomplish right away, and make even small progress?" By setting smaller, short-range goals, over time you can complete the list. Your hope is restored that you won't be overwhelmed for the rest of your life, and the depression often lets up.

Do I need to get away?

Getting away from everything, even for just an hour, can restore your hope. So decide immediately when and where to go, and take that needed break.

To whom could I offer a meaningful gift?

Depression is often self-centered. If you're depressed today, you may think you don't need to hear that. But often the best way to lift yourself out of depression is to find out something meaningful that someone else wants or needs, and give it to them. Move away from self-focus and get your focus on others.

What you need most today may be what you haven't given freely enough in the past. For example, if you feel you need encouragement, ask yourself, "Have I been encouraging others lately?"

Remember

In the future, should you ever need to overcome depression, turn to this chapter and ask yourself these critical questions:

- Why am I depressed?
- What specific things are weighing heavily on me today?
- Am I angry at anyone?
- Am I physically or mentally fatigued?
- Have I been experiencing too much change too fast?
- Am I seeing my situation with a long-term perspective?
- Do I have clear and meaningful goals for the future?
- What milestones in my past can cheer me up at this time?
- What friend can I call to cheer me up at this time?
- What positive, specific step can I take right now—no matter how small?
- Do I need to get away?
- To whom could I offer a meaningful gift?

Knowing the right questions can mean the critical difference in increasing your leadership confidence.

11 DISCIPLINE

Everyone wants to be thin, but no one wants to diet. Everybody wants money, but not many want to work hard. Lots of people like a nice yard or garden, but few like pulling weeds.

Discipline is the means to getting what you really want. And yet often, even when we know clearly what we want and we strive to be disciplined to attain it, we still falter in our discipline. I'm sure you know what I mean.

At times I've shocked people with this statement: "*Discipline* is not your problem; *motivation* is!" Discipline and motivation are two sides of the same coin. If you have the motivation you need, discipline is no problem. If you lack motivation, discipline is always a problem.

For example, if you have children in school who have trouble getting up and ready on a normal school day, you may have noticed that the problem disappears the day of the school picnic or a field trip to an amusement park.

In this chapter, therefore, I'll actually talk less about discipline and more about the *motivation* that will increase your discipline.

In what area of your life would you like to be more disciplined? Whatever it is, if you approach that problem area by telling yourself, "I've got to be more disciplined, I've got to be more disciplined, I've got to more disciplined," I predict that you'll continually experience struggles and disappointment. But if I can help you find the proper motivation, discipline in that area of your life will become a natural by-product.

Before I begin sounding as if I'm offering a magic elixir to solve your discipline problems overnight, I must confess that I know what the battle for discipline is like. It's a struggle for me in many areas of my life. I know there are no easy answers for having a perfect body, a perfect lawn, or a perfect life. It just isn't easy to be disciplined.

But I've found that the following questions help increase my discipline by clarifying my motivation.

Do I have clear goals that are pulling me into the future?

As we saw in chapter 5 on "Communication," we weigh value/price considerations in every decision we make. If the price is too high for the value we receive, we don't pay the price.

It's the same with discipline. Without an adequate answer to the question, "Why should I do it?" we won't run the extra lap, we won't say no to the extra piece of cake. The only thing that makes discipline worthwhile is having a clear idea of what we want to achieve by the discipline. Discipline is not the end, but a means to something we want. And unless what we want is clear enough to us, we won't have discipline to achieve it.

> If hard work is the key to success,
> most people would rather pick the lock.
> —*William Gladstone*
>
> Choose a job you love, and you'll never have
> to work a day in your life.
> —*Confucius*

Are your goals urgent enough, vivid enough, and clear enough that you can say no to things today in order to achieve those goals in the future? If your goals aren't clear, or if you say, "Bobb, I don't really have any goals for the future," then don't be surprised when your discipline sags.

Do I truly understand *why* I want to achieve these goals? And are these reasons constantly before me, for my inspiration?

"Bobb," you may say, "what I really want is a new boat, so I'm disciplining my spending to save for it." That's your goal. But *why* do you want the boat? Maybe it's for the special peace and contentment you feel on fishing trips up the river, or the fun of waterskiing on the lake. Or maybe it's because you want people to see you in that boat and think about how successful you are. Whatever it is, the *why* is even more critically important than the *what.*

Am I growing personally?

When you have a sense of personally maturing, of becoming better than you were last month or last year, it brings an extra capacity for discipline in continuing to grow.

Is discipline missing in a certain area of my life? Why?

Pinpoint your area of weakness, and examine the facts. Exactly what have you done or failed to do?

If discipline is missing in a certain area of my life, what are the possible or probable consequences if I don't restore or develop it?

If you don't develop an exercise program and lose some weight, will it set you up for an early heart attack? If you don't start saving more, will you have to scale down that dream vacation you planned to take next summer?

Can I stay disciplined even when no one else notices?

You can't be consistent in discipline if it depends on other people watching and admiring you. There are just too many occasions when you have to take a step of discipline alone, when no one else is around. Your motivation for discipline must come from *within.*

How can I approach discipline in a step-by-step, achievable manner?

If you're exercising by swimming, keep a chart to record how many laps you swim each time (and watch the miles add up over time). If you're dieting, weigh yourself at least every other day.

> It takes six weeks to establish a habit.
> Most of us quit just short of the goal.

Who can I team up with for mutual encouragement?

The vice-president of a company I worked for used to tell me, "Alone you're alone, but two people make a team." If you're alone on your diet, alone in your dreams and goals, alone with your plans, then you're truly alone. The step of discipline seems like such a big jump. With just one other person, however, you've got help when you get down or discouraged or overwhelmed. You have someone to remind you of what you want and why you want it—someone to help you "keep on keeping on!"

Remember

In the future, whenever you feel your discipline slackening, ask yourself these essential questions:

- Do I have clear goals that are pulling me into the future?
- Do I truly understand *why* I want to achieve these goals? And are these reasons constantly before me, for my inspiration?
- Am I growing personally?
- Is discipline missing in a certain area of my life? Why?
- If discipline is missing in a certain area of my life, what are the possible or probable consequences if I don't restore or develop it?
- Can I stay disciplined even when no one else notices?
- How can I approach discipline in a step-by-step, achievable manner?
- Who can I team up with for mutual encouragement?

Asking the right questions can increase your motivation, strengthen your discipline, and increase your leadership confidence.

12 DREAMING

Do you see yourself as a visionary?

For our discussion here, *your vision or dream is simply your view of what life would be like if certain current needs were met.* You are a "visionary" if you can *see* what difference it would make, even though it doesn't yet exist.

Your dreams are like a huge motivational magnet. They help pull you through life's low points.

Dreaming is necessary, not only personally, but also on the corporate and organizational level. *The company that doesn't commit at least a small percentage of its time to simply reflect and see new possibilities is doomed to maintaining the status quo.*

If you're a corporate or organizational leader, set aside time to meet with your staff and begin imagining twenty years into the future. Then ask yourselves, *As a team, what must we do to prepare for the challenges of the next twenty years?*

The more you care about being a vital corporation twenty years from now, the more you'll take time today to get ready for that coming reality.

Use the following questions to sharpen your dreams and move toward turning them into reality.

What goal or cause or dream do I believe in deeply enough to die for?

What do you care deeply about today? What do you want to do and keep doing? What needs do you feel so strongly about that you would give your life to help meet them? If you're willing to die for them, you're probably also willing to give the rest of your life to see that those needs are met long-term.

The dream you give your life to may not be yours alone. In fact, your dream could help someone else reach his or her dream, if, in fact, you share that person's thinking.

What single need do I care most strongly about today?

In all that you identified in the question above, what is the most prominent need? This is the starting point for your dream. The broader and deeper the need, the higher your dream's potential.

If you see no need, you will have no dream. So if you don't have a dream, look for a big need that ought to be met. Once you recognize the need, think about it, commit yourself to meeting it, and plan for it—then you have your dream.

What am I uniquely equipped and positioned to accomplish?

This factor is frequently called your "Unique Market Position." You want to identify not only the things you're deeply concerned about but also those things that, because of your background, training, or other factors, you are in a unique position to do something about today.

> I have been trying all my life, first to see for myself, and then to get other people to see with me. To succeed in business it is necessary to make the other man see things as you see them. Seeing . . . was the objective. In the broadest possible sense, I am a visualizer.
>
> —*John W. Patterson*
> (founder of National Cash Register)

You may care deeply for hungry children on a different continent, but you have no way of getting there and providing direct help. You may also care deeply for needy children in your own city whom you could actually help.

Because of who you are, where you are, or the resources you have, what is your unique opportunity?

> A man tends to overestimate what he
> can do in a year . . .
> And underestimate what he can do in five.
> —*Dr. Ted. W. Engstrom*

What are the long-term implications of accomplishing my dream?

As you work to carry out your dream, what difference will it make fifty or one hundred or five hundred years from now?

Keep in mind the difference between a winner's and a loser's mentality: winners focus on *winning big*—not just how to win, but how to win big. Losers, however, don't focus on losing; they just focus on getting by.

Keep asking yourself, *Survival, success, or significance?* Are we striving to simply survive, are we dreaming about success, or are we really out to make a truly significant difference?

Moshe Rosen teaches a one-sentence mental exercise that's an effective tool in dreaming:

If I had ________________________________,
I would ________________________________.

If you had anything you wanted—unlimited time, unlimited money, unlimited information, unlimited staff—all the resources you could ask for—what would you do? Your answer to that question is your dream.

What if my dream is a hundred times more successful than I plan?

In other words, be ready. Know how to stay with your dream if it experiences explosive growth.

Have I asked myself the Mind-Stretcher Questions?

These questions on page 12 can help give you different perspectives on how to meet the need you want to meet, which in turn begins to clarify new possibilities and options you haven't seen before.

In your company, your organization, or your department, perhaps it's time for a brainstorming session on the topics that need totally new solutions. Make a list of them and prioritize them; then take them one area at a time, one project at a time, one step at a time, and ask the Mind-Stretcher Questions about each one.

Use the process to stimulate new concepts and dreams. Otherwise you may be forfeiting progress by getting trapped in an ingrown, subjective, day-to-day perspective.

As you build your dreams, take a look also at whatever worked better this year than you thought it would—something that was more productive or profitable or popular than you expected. Ask how you could make it a hundred times more productive next year. Peter Drucker puts it this way: "See this year's unexpected successes as next year's opportunities." Start dreaming about the possibilities.

Could someone else with an objective viewpoint help me see possibilities that I have been missing?

Here's where the objectivity of an outside consultant often plays a vital role in seeing totally new solutions.

Frequently, a few new questions, a new set of ears, and a fresh look uncover "gold lying on the ground."

What successful models from the past may have something to say to me now?

Finally, I challenge you to think so big that you can't possibly accomplish your dreams alone—so big that you can't accomplish your dreams this year, this decade, or even in your lifetime. Have a dream worth dreaming, a challenge so big that even getting recognition for it is unnecessary.

In my experience working with executives year after year, I've found that a person often performs his work primarily to hear people say, "You've done a good job." But a hundred years from now, who will care whether we lived or died? Fame is fleeting. You must have a dream that's big enough to transcend the issue of who gets credit for it.

Most of us have vast potential that has never been developed simply because we have failed to realize it, or the circumstances of our lives have never required it. *Start dreaming and keep dreaming;* and if your dream ever gets dim or foggy, take a long look at these questions again to sharpen your vision.

> In working closely with leaders,
> I have often asked myself,
> Does the man make the dream?
> Or does the dream make the man?
> My conclusion: *Both are equally true!*

REMEMBER

In the future, when your dreams need reshaping, refocusing, or refining, turn to this chapter and ask yourself these questions:

- What goal or cause or dream do I believe in deeply enough to die for?
- What single need do I care most strongly about today?
- What am I uniquely equipped and positioned to accomplish?
- What are the long-term implications of accomplishing my dream?
- What if my dream is a hundred times more successful than I plan?
- Have I asked myself the Mind-Stretcher Questions?
- Could someone else with an objective viewpoint help me see possibilities that I have been missing?
- What successful models from the past may have something to say to me now?

You'll build both your dreams and your leadership confidence by knowing and asking the right questions.

13 FAILURE

You've probably known that sickening feeling: You think everyone in the world must know you've failed, and you have to force yourself just to keep your head up.

What's been the biggest failure of your life? Maybe it was seeing a company go bankrupt because of your unwise decisions, or seeing your marriage end in divorce. Perhaps it was failing a professional examination, or being fired from the position you worked a lifetime to get.

Whatever it was, have you overcome the sense of injury it caused? Have you resolved any lingering negative emotions and questions?

In this chapter I'd like to help you go back through any experiences of failure you've known, and offer helpful questions for you and also for any friend of yours who may be overwhelmed by feelings of failure.

These are valuable questions for your future, because any growing person who continues the healthy process of attempting new challenges in life will find failure at some point.

> A mistake at least proves that somebody
> stopped talking long enough
> to do something.
> —from *Apples of Gold*

Did I fail because of another person, because of my situation, or because of myself?

Most adults tend to assume major responsibility for failures they were involved in, when in fact it may not have been their fault at all.

Although the failure you have in mind at the moment is probably one that you believe was your fault, actually you may have teamed up with someone else—a manager or partner or friend—with whom it was basically impossible to win. If the presidents of the nation's fifty largest companies had each teamed up with that person, they might have all failed too. Your failure may have been, in large part, the other person's responsibility.

This is often true when the failure occurred in your teenage or early adult years. Maybe you're looking back and saying, "My greatest failure was when I was sixteen and I had my first job: the boss yelled at me, fired me, and threw me out of the store" or some similar incident.

Your immaturity at the time was certainly a factor, but the person you were dealing with may have had a big share of the blame as well.

Look back at the incident as an adult now, rather than through the emotional eyes of a youth, and see if that doesn't make sense.

Another reality is that the *situation* you were in may have caused the failure. Maybe you tried to do something that no one could have done; you set goals that were impossible. Maybe you tried to turn around a company that was simply too far gone, and the most skillful turn-around team in the world couldn't have saved it.

Or maybe the fault was, in fact, with you. If so, then say to yourself, "All right, what did I learn? And what else do I need to learn to keep from failing like that in the future?"

Did I actually fail, or did I simply fall short of an unrealistically high standard?

In your experience of failure, did you expect yourself to be perfect? Sometimes we have unreasonably high expectations or standards, and if we fall a little short of them, we may think we're failures. Has that been the situation in your case?

If so, I have good news:

- It's *OK* to be less than perfect.
- You do *not* have to reach every goal.
- And you *don't* have to be perfect to be *extremely significant.*

> I cannot give you a formula for success,
> but I can give you the formula for failure:
> Try to please everybody.
> —*Herbert Bayard Swope*

I'm good at goal setting. I've set many goals, and reached many. But I don't reach all the goals I set, nor do I feel like a failure because I haven't reached them. Some of the goals turned out to be unrealistic in light of new realities, such as different responsibilities. Sometimes it becomes obvious that a goal is simply no longer important, so I abandon it.

Where did I succeed, as well as fail?

Many people who experience a major failure tend to have blurred memories about the things they actually did right in the situation. They focus only on the few things they did wrong that caused the emotionally traumatic feeling of failure.

As you think back on your own experience of failure, make a list of all the ways in which you feel you succeeded or did what was right in that situation.

> Only a mediocre person
> is always at his best.
> —*W. Somerset Maugham*

What lessons have I learned?

Maybe you've learned not to jump too quickly into something, or to seek harder for wise counsel from other people.

> Failure isn't failure
> unless you don't learn from it.
> —*Dr. Roland Niednagel*

Am I grateful for this experience?

You can't resent something for which you're truly thankful. If you're overwhelmed and intimidated by that failure of the past, you can't be thankful for it. If you are thankful for it, you see its value in your life.

If it looms in your memory as a great failure that continues to affect you emotionally, let me suggest that others involved have probably long since forgotten.

Maybe you recall a quick, unthinking remark by a teacher—"That was the worst paper I've ever received"—and you've carried the memory into your adulthood. You are probably the only one who remembers that failure.

Forgive, forget, and move on!

How can I turn the failure into success?

How can yesterday's failure be a part of your success today? How can you turn lemons into lemonade? What have you learned that you can now pass on to others?

Practically speaking, where do I go from here?

What are your plans? When? How?

Who else has failed in this way before, and how can they help me?

Often, just talking with someone who has also failed in this area can help you gain perspective on what went wrong. Do you know someone like that?

How can my experience help others someday to keep from failing?

Can you give a helpful warning to others by telling them of your own failure?

Finally, listen to these words from Abraham Lincoln:

> I do the very best I know how—the very best I can—and mean to keep doing so until the end. If the end brings me out right, what is said against me won't amount to anything. If the end brings me out wrong, ten angels swearing I was right would make no difference.

Do your best. Do what you think is right. But you can't win 'em all. When you do fail, look again at the questions in this chapter and let them help you bounce back better than ever.

REMEMBER

In the future, whenever you or a friend is stalked by a sense of failure, turn to this chapter and let these questions turn your thoughts in the right direction:

- Did I fail because of another person, because of my situation, or because of myself?
- Did I actually fail, or did I simply fall short of an unrealistically high standard?
- Where did I succeed, as well as fail?
- What lessons have I learned?
- Am I grateful for this experience?
- How can I turn the failure into success?
- Practically speaking, where do I go from here?
- Who else has failed in this way before, and how can they help me?
- How can my experience help others someday to keep from failing?

When you're facing failure, knowing the right questions helps you turn it into success, building your leadership confidence.

14 FATIGUE

Fatigue makes us introspective and negative. It eats away our confidence. Even the leader who is normally positive and confident will become unsure of himself in a state of deep fatigue.

> Fatigue makes cowards of us all.
> —*Vince Lombardi*

If you're feeling fatigued today—weary, worn, burned out, "bedraggled" as my grandmother used to say—you'll have an unrealistic perspective of situations requiring your leadership, and you won't be as competent as you could and should be.

Here are questions to help you gain perspective on how to move from a state of fatigue to a state of rest:

How can I get an extra ten hours of sleep as soon as possible?

Frequently the best prescription for fatigue is just to sleep every spare minute until we are fully rested—no television, no sports, no social life, no hobbies, no extra volunteer assignments—only *sleep!*

I've had probably a hundred executives tell me, "Just having had a good night's sleep made all the difference." They had been trying to solve a problem or get on top of a situation, and had just gotten weary. After a good night's rest, they were eager to tackle the problem that had seemed so intimidating the night before.

How quickly can you get ten hours of sleep beyond your normal sleep time? It may take a week, but try it, and watch your level of confidence (and competence) grow.

What things are weighing heavily on my shoulders?

Make a complete list of all your responsibilities, large and small. Get them out of your mind for the time being, and onto paper. Then get a good night's rest. (To handle the list you come up with, you may want to look at chap. 25 on "Prioritizing.") Tell yourself, *I can deal with this list tomorrow. Tonight I'm just going to sleep.*

Over the past ten years I've given this assignment personally to perhaps a hundred individuals. It may surprise you to learn that their average list contained fifty to seventy-five items, most being what you could reasonably call "little things." When we're in a state of fatigue, often we feel overwhelmed by the number of these "little things." Any one of them we could do easily, but when we carry around the weight of them all—"I should do these projects, and call these contacts, and visit these people," and dozens more items—it takes so much energy that soon we feel we can't take another step. That's fatigue.

Do I have clear, meaningful, and achievable goals?

A word of caution, especially when you're in a state of fatigue: Don't set too many goals. Set short-term goals, things you can get done this week, or today. Also set low, measurable goals that you know you can reach even though you're tired. When you've accomplished them, you'll say to yourself, *I've actually succeeded today in doing this and this and this.*

Is my focus in life on *efficiency* or *effectiveness?*

Peter Drucker defines *efficiency* as "doing things right," and *effectiveness* as "doing the right things." Which is your focus?

If you focus on doing things right, but you're doing the wrong things, you'll frequently realize at the end of a busy day or week that you've left the truly important tasks undone. So keep asking yourself, "Is what I am doing the thing I *should* be doing?"

Again, chapter 25 on "Prioritizing" can be a big help. You can go through that list of seventy-five things and distinguish between "What I really *have* to do" and "What I would *like* to do but don't really have to." The items in the second category are the ones you can scratch out on your list and say to yourself, "When I finish everything else and get my sleep, I may want to come back and pick up some of those things; but for now, I'm taking them *off* my 'to-do' list." Or, for some of them you may decide, "I'm just not going to do that, period." Forget about them.

In your volunteer activities, evaluating your effectiveness means asking, "In which one or two or three of these activities am I truly making a big contribution?" Focus your attention on the few that you can really make a difference in, and let go of the others that are just taking up your time, energy, and money.

Am I in good physical condition?

When you're out of shape, it can take twice the time and energy to accomplish what you do.

Are you overweight—and therefore exerting the extra energy it takes to carry that weight around all day? A friend of mine says that if he gets ten pounds overweight, when he goes grocery shopping he picks up a ten-pound bag of sugar and carries it with him as he shops, just to feel how tiring it is to carry around those extra pounds.

Am I living on "natural" energy or "forced" energy?

We exert natural energy when doing something we *want* to do; forced energy is what drives us when we feel we *have* to do something. Operating on forced energy is twice as tiring—and only half as effective—as natural energy.

Are you forcing yourself to do what you're doing in life, or are you doing it because you want to?

Do I feel I am growing personally?

When you have a sense of growing, everything seems more exciting, even when you're tired.

How can I approach my future work one step at a time?

If you could do only one thing today, what would you do? If you could do only one thing this week, what would it be? If you could do only one thing this year, what would it be?

What responsibilities can I delegate to others?

Fatigue can be fundamentally an *organizational* issue—it's not having the right team in place. The person with the right team can do the appropriate amount of work and leave the rest of the work to other people.

What items on your list could someone else do at least 80 percent as well as you? Doing these things yourself is probably a waste of your time. (See chap. 9 to learn how to delegate effectively.)

What Mind-Stretcher Questions should I be asking?

We keep coming back to these questions from page 12, but they can be extremely useful, especially if you keep thinking about them often enough so that your mind returns to them automatically in various situations in life.

Remember

Whenever you feel fatigued or burned out, let these questions help you regain vitality:

- How can I get an extra ten hours of sleep as soon as possible?
- What things are weighing heavily on my shoulders?
- Do I have clear, meaningful, and achievable goals?
- Is my focus in life on *efficiency* (doing things right) or *effectiveness* (doing the right things)?
- Am I in good physical condition?
- Am I living on "natural" energy or "forced" energy?
- Do I feel I am growing personally?
- How can I approach my future work one step at a time?
- What responsibilities can I delegate to others?
- What Mind-Stretcher Questions should I be asking?

By knowing and asking the right questions when you experience fatigue, you'll increase your leadership confidence.

15 FIRING

"I've been *fired.*" What terrifying words! And almost equally as terrifying is the statement, "I think we're going to have to fire so-and-so." For most executives, having to fire a staff member is the single most difficult aspect of their leadership.

How can it be done in the right way? I believe the essence of doing it right is in maintaining this perspective: *When you appropriately fire a person from a position in which he is failing, you are actually releasing him from that failure—and freeing him to seek a position in which he can find success.* With a proper release, it's even possible to instill in the person the excitement that comes from anticipating a new venture.

In a sense, you are telling the person, "I've got good news: I'm going to release you from this failure situation, and activate the process of finding you a new and more fulfilling position."

"Bobb," you may be saying, "with that kind of idealism, you obviously have never fired anyone!" Actually I've been a part of "releasing" about a hundred executives, and I can testify that it is *never* easy. But I'm convinced from experience that the right perspective is to see it as that person's release *from* failure and *to* a more fulfilling position.

The following questions can help you maintain that needed viewpoint:

Does this person clearly understand the role, goals, responsibilities, and standards for his or her position?

If the person doesn't have this clear understanding, the lack of performance you see may simply be a matter of not knowing what you want done.

If you have clear, specific standards for the job, it makes releasing someone ten times easier.

Why is the person not performing adequately?

Is it because of a:

lack of *training?*

lack of *motivation?*

lack of *experience?*

lack of *ability?*

lack of *clear assignment?*

Why is it? Explore all five of these possibilities before making your conclusion.

What would be the benefits of having this person stay in the position?

Make a list of the advantages of keeping this person, such as not having downtime in the position, not having to find and train a replacement, and so on. You can weigh these factors against whatever you perceive as the person's shortcomings: his lack of training, experience, ability, or motivation.

What would be the difficulties associated with having this person stay in the position?

Is there a possibility of helping this person be successful in this position sometime in the future? If not, move him—and, within reason, the sooner, the better (as a rule of thumb). Once you decide in your mind that "this person will never make it in this job," release him today instead of next month so he has an additional thirty days of his life to be looking for a position that better suits him.

If you feel someone isn't doing what he should, but you don't address that immediately, you'll soon begin to resent that person's being there—"I'm paying him, but he isn't performing." You can actually be angry that he's still there, and these emotions will cloud the issue.

On the other hand, be sensitive to his life situation. Another rule of thumb is to treat an employee you're releasing as you would want your father, mother, brother, or sister to be treated.

What psychological dynamics are involved in this person's staying or leaving?

Ask questions such as, "What will other staff members think?" "What sense of loss will the person's spouse experience, and what will be the impact on the children?" It may be good to write down your thoughts on these factors before making a final decision concerning the person's future.

Can this person be transferred to a different position? If so, what would be the associated advantages and difficulties?

A person who isn't performing well in one position within a company or organization may be a big winner in another. To use a football analogy, the man who isn't a good quarterback may still be an all-star defensive player, and vice versa.

How do I feel about this person? And what feelings about the person are other team members experiencing?

Get in touch with these feelings. Ask yourself, "Am I angry with this person, or am I being objective?"

You may need someone from the outside to help give you objectivity—another staff member, someone from another department or division, or a consultant. Tell the outsider, "I'm angry with this person, and I'm afraid I've lost my objectivity. Help me get a clear picture."

Am I committed to this person's success?

Do I care about this person enough to ask him to find other work where he can be more successful?

What further questions must be answered before I will know whether he or she should go or stay?

In a potential firing, there always seem to be a few lingering questions that keep you from being totally sure about whether to let the person go. Get these on paper and answer them before you make the final decision.

What recognition does this person deserve?

If *you* were being released, what recognition would you want?

You may feel that "outstanding performance" recognition is inappropriate for someone being released. You may fear that when you award recognition, others will think, "If he's that good, why are they letting him go?" Or you may think it implies that the person's performance was fully satisfactory, when in fact it wasn't.

But understand that this person has given part of his life to help in your company or department or organization, and whatever things he did right are what you want to recognize him for. Make the effort to say "thank you" in a meaningful way.

You may find it wise to focus your comments on the person's positive attitude or character traits rather than his performance.

Again, treat any person leaving your organization as you would want someone to treat one of your own family members—especially on the day he leaves.

Remember

If you may have to fire someone, turn to these questions to get a clear perspective:

- Does this person clearly understand the role, goals, responsibilities, and standards for his or her position?
- Why is the person not performing adequately?
- What would be the benefits of having this person stay in the position?
- What would be the difficulties associated with having this person stay in the position?
- What psychological dynamics are involved in this person's staying or leaving?
- Can this person be transferred to a different position? If so, what would be the associated advantages and difficulties?
- How do I feel about this person? What feelings about the person are other team members experiencing?
- Am I committed to this person's success?
- What further questions must be answered before I will know whether he or she should go or stay?
- What recognition does this person deserve?

In a situation as difficult as firing someone, knowing the right questions is a key to increasing your leadership confidence.

16 GOAL SETTING

Success can be defined as the feeling you get when you reach your goals. That's why, for many leaders, that little word *goals* connotes success. But that's also why, for others, the very mention of the word *goals* feels emotionally like failure.

In a seminar for leaders, I once passed around slips of paper and asked everyone to answer yes or no to this question: "Do *goals* equal *failure* in your emotional system?" Thirty percent of these leaders answered yes.

That's why setting appropriate goals is such an important factor in leadership confidence. *When realistic goals are set and met, you'll feel successful,* and the whole concept of setting goals will have the exciting flavor of accomplishment.

Another important reason for setting goals is that it transitions you from daily details to more long-term priorities. You switch from fire fighting to fire prevention—from simply responding to the urgent to managing the important.

Here are some of the most profound questions I know to help you set goals successfully:

What needs do I care most deeply about meeting?

Set your goals in areas that are meaningful to you emotionally.

What is my life focus?

On the next two pages is a "Life Focus Chart" to complete—four categories, each containing ten boxes. Ask yourself:

1. Between now and the time I die, what are the ten things I want to *be?* In this column you can list such things as "a successful parent" or "a good friend," or character traits such as "honest," "loyal," or "teachable." This column should reflect your highest values.
2. Between now and the time I die, what are the ten things I want to *do?* This column should be a list of measurable things you want to accomplish.
3. Between now and the time I die, what are the ten things I want to *have?*
4. Between now and the time I die, who are the ten individuals or groups I want to *help?*

By completing this list you'll have a fuller context for making day-to-day goal setting more meaningful. You can build a step-by-step bridge from where you are today to the lifetime accomplishments listed in your chart.

The ten things I want to **BE**	The ten things I want to **DO**

The ten things I want to **HAVE**	The ten people or groups I want to **HELP**

In the diagram below you can see the words *objective, goals,* and *purpose.* These words have a variety of definitions in use today, so it's important that everyone on your team uses them in the same way as you make plans and set goals.

The following questions and explanations will indicate how these three terms are used in this chapter.

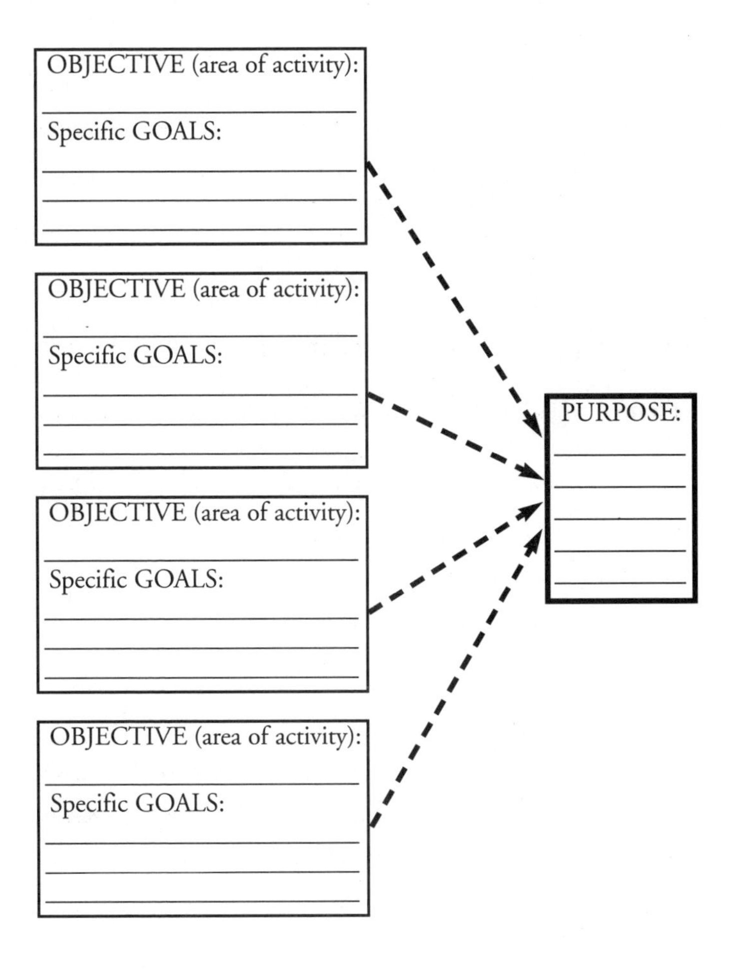

Why am I here? (What is my *purpose?*)

On a personal level, the question is "Why do I exist?" You can also ask it on a group level: "Why does this company (or "this organization" or "this department") exist?" Your answer is your purpose statement. It is not a measurable goal. Rather, it's more like the North Star. It's something you are moving toward.

For example, my company's purpose is "to maximize the leadership ability of our clients." For decade after decade, that's what we intend to do. We'll never complete the job, but it's a statement that, like the North Star, is always there to give us direction.

In what three to seven areas will I continue to concentrate my energy over the next five to ten years? (What are my *objectives?*)

Once you've defined your purpose by answering the question "Why do I exist?" you should decide what categories of activity you'll be involved in as you move toward your purpose.

In my firm, these broad areas of activity include consulting services, seminars, and personal growth resources (such as books and tapes).

On a personal level, you could list your objective areas as the seven basic areas of life we discussed in chapter 3: family and marriage, financial, personal growth, physical, professional, social, and spiritual.

What three specific and measurable things will I do this year in each area of my objectives? (What are my *goals?*)

Here we get into measurability. Your goals are the specific, measurable things you want to accomplish. You should have measurable goals in each of your objective areas. But don't set too many, or you'll be overwhelmed.

Again on a personal level, you can list a few goals in each of the seven basic areas of life.

As you reach these goals, you'll feel successful. If you don't reach them, you won't feel as successful. But remember—you don't have to reach them all in order to make a major difference. You can do extremely significant things even if you reach only half your goals.

Why do I want to accomplish these objectives and goals?

As you set your goals, ask yourself, "Why do I want to reach this goal?" If you can't come up with an adequate answer, the price you have to pay to reach that goal—in time, energy, or money—will be too high.

What will happen if I do *not* reach my goals?

Think through this question for every goal you set. Sometimes the result of not reaching a goal could be disastrous. Other goals are less significant.

Do I need to set goals that are more realistically attainable?

Maybe you need to set lower goals because you've always felt like a failure after not attaining goals that were set too high.

Beware especially of setting unrealistic goals when: (1) you have no proven track record in an area, (2) you're in an extreme emotional state (as when you're so excited that you think nothing is impossible), (3) you're only trying to impress the boss (it's better to impress him with results than with goals, especially when those goals could make you look like a failure three months from now), and (4) the final results depend on others who may not do their part.

Who can help me be accountable for my goals?

Someone else who knows and supports your goals can be your team member in helping you achieve them.

How will I reward myself when I reach each goal?

Attach a reward to the accomplishment—something that's enjoyable as well as good for you.

Remember

Ask yourself these foundational questions to help you set clear, motivating, achievable goals:

- What needs do I care most deeply about meeting?
- What is my life focus?
- Why am I here? (What is my *purpose?*)
- In what three to seven areas will I continue to concentrate my energy over the next five to ten years? (What are my *objectives?*)
- What three specific and measurable things will I do this year in each area of my objectives? (What are my *goals?*)
- *Why* do I want to accomplish these objectives and goals?
- What will happen if I do *not* reach my goals?
- Do I need to set goals that are more realistically attainable?
- Who can help me be accountable for my goals?
- How will I reward myself when I reach each goal?

When you ask the right questions, you can set realistic goals and enjoy a feeling of success, increasing your leadership confidence.

17 INFLUENCING

On the first anniversary of the creation of the citizens' group Common Cause, founder John W. Gardner wrote a summary of the rules this group had learned for influencing decision makers and accomplishing change. Included were:

- Limit the number of targets, and hit them hard.
- Put a professional cutting edge on citizen enthusiasm.
- Form alliances.
- Tell the story.

By following these and other fundamental rules, Common Cause in its first year grew to include 250,000 members (its first-year target was only 25,000), and it continues to be an effective citizens' voice for influencing public policies.

Your experience in influencing major decisions made by others—whether in government, in business, among your professional colleagues or your friends, or in some other arena—can in its own way be just as successful as Common Cause's.

The following questions can help you focus your influencing energy:

What do I consider to be the three most important decisions to be made by other people in the near future?

Concentrate your energy on a few key targets. For every potential target, ask yourself, "What will be the five- to fifty-year impact of this decision? What difference will it make?" One decision might make a two-year difference, another a ten-year difference, and another a fifty-year difference.

This kind of evaluation can help you decide in which areas to invest your time, energy, and money.

Why do I want to influence these particular decisions?

Is it for the good of my children and their children? Is it for my own recognition? Is it for my country? Is it because of my faith in God? Is it just to see things change? Why do I want so strongly to influence this issue?

Who will actually be making these decisions? And how can I influence them?

To influence a group, in most cases you need only to influence the one or two most dominant people in the group. Who are they? How can you influence them?

Am I committed to the best interests of these people? And how can I communicate that commitment?

Abraham Lincoln said, "Before you can convince a man of anything, you must first convince him that you are his true friend."

Take thirty seconds right now to think back on the times in your life when you've changed your mind about something major. Isn't it true that a *friend* was instrumental in that change? We all learn from our friends. When supportive friends try to influence us, we change.

Are you a true friend to the people you want to influence? If so, how can you convince them of your friendship? Don't play a con game, but if you really are on their side, how can you demonstrate it?

You may at times find yourself in a tug-of-war—a potential argument—with the people you want to influence. When that happens, instead of trying to argue against them, argue *with* them *against the problem.* You'll find more acceptance for your ideas.

If instead you try to prove them wrong—if your desire is to mentally arm wrestle them to the table, to hear their knuckles crack, to hear them beg for mercy—you'll only meet resistance. But if you can get on their end of the struggle and say, "I see why you're so concerned with this. Let me help you solve the problem," their response will be positive.

What facts should these people be aware of before making these decisions?

To again quote Peter Drucker, "Once the facts are clear, the decisions jump out at you." Find out what facts the decision maker needs for making the decision—then supply those facts.

Have I done my homework?

I once asked a venture capitalist with majority holdings in a few dozen companies—a man who had sat on thirty to fifty boards at various times—"What is the secret of being a good board member?"

"It's very simple," he replied. "Do your homework. In most of the board meetings I attend, the members simply arrive, open their file, and start looking for where they left off the previous month. They aren't prepared to really influence because they haven't done their homework."

What are the value/price considerations in these decisions?

Think again about the value/price factors discussed in chapter 5. Make sure you communicate the value of the decision you're suggesting and the cost involved in going a different direction.

Who else wants to influence these decisions?

With whom can you cooperate? Find someone who shares your goals and form an alliance.

How can I invest money wisely to provide influence?

What organizations do you want to win? Extend their influence by helping provide adequate funding for them.

A final question:

How will these decisions affect each person involved?

REMEMBER

To know how to influence those whose decisions mean the most to you, ask yourself these questions:

- What do I consider to be the three most important decisions to be made by other people in the near future?
- *Why* do I want to influence these particular decisions?
- *Who* will actually be making these decisions? And how can I influence them?
- Am I committed to the best interests of these people? And how can I communicate that commitment?
- What facts should these people be aware of before making these decisions?
- Have I done my homework?
- What are the value/price considerations in these decisions?
- Who else wants to influence these decisions?
- How can I invest money wisely to provide influence?
- How will these decisions affect each person involved?

Knowing the right questions gives you greater influence and helps increase your leadership confidence.

18 MASTERPLANNING

A masterplan is simply a written statement that tells a group's assumptions about its direction, its organization, and its resources.

A masterplan's greatest benefit is in providing a unified set of plans for all levels of leadership within an organization—in other words, it allows everyone to be playing from the same sheet of music. A masterplan provides:

- A common plan that the entire team can be a part of
- A solid foundation for creating and refining a team environment
- A shared basis for clear decision making
- A basic context for problem solving
- A communications framework that the entire staff can use for telling outsiders "who we are"
- A planning model that allows fast growth without "killing" the organization

A company or organization that does not have a masterplan is likely to suffer these symptoms:

- Foggy communications
- Frustration and tension arising from different assumptions about who's responsible for what, who's responsible to whom, how much is available for what, and so on
- Delayed decisions
- Wasted energy and resources
- Inadequate funding
- Diminished quality of service
- Vagueness about the future
- Inadequate preparation for growth

Developing a masterplan means dealing with at least the following ten questions:

Who are we trying to serve, and what needs are we meeting? (Market)

Who is your market and what is their need? Without a need to fill, you have no reason to exist.

Do we have the right people at the top to accomplish our goals? (Leadership)

You can have a great plan for meeting a big need, but without the right leadership, you're unlikely to make it happen.

Whose advice do we need in order to succeed? (Counsel)

Your advisers might be a board of directors, an advisory council, a steering committee, or outside consultants. What resources of expertise outside your organization do you need to have access to in order to plan and succeed?

Exactly what are we going to do short-range, mid-range, and long-range? (Direction)

After you have identified your market and its needs, and your leadership and counsel are in place, the next step is to decide what direction you'll take.

Now you have a clear direction, you know where you're going as a company or organization. You can now define:

Who will be responsible for what? And who will be responsible for whom? (Organization)

Do you have the right people in place? (See chap. 27 on "Recruiting" for help in this area.)

What are our expected expenses and income? (Cash)

How much will it cost and can you afford it?

Once you have your leadership, direction, organization, and working capital, you have at least 80 percent of what you need to lead effectively. Now you can focus on:

Are we on target? (Reporting)

In this step are the six questions every staff member should be able to answer for you (see chap. 28 on "Reporting").

How can we effectively make known what we're doing? (Communication)

This involves both internal communication as well as external.

Are we seeing the quality we expect or demand from ourselves? (Evaluating)

Evaluate people, programs, and overall organization.

And finally,

How can we keep improving in the critical aspects of this project or service? (Refining)

A masterplan is typically put together in a team effort; in fact, masterplanning is a *process* that will help develop a group's team spirit.

The best times to create a masterplan are when you're starting something new, when you're going through major changes, or when your previous masterplan was done either too long ago or never.

Masterplanning is not a task to do only once every five or ten years, but a process to be involved in continually.

REMEMBER

Turn to this chapter to find the key questions involved in the masterplanning process:

- Who are we trying to serve, and what needs are we meeting? (Market)
- Do we have the right people at the top to accomplish our goals? (Leadership)
- Whose advice do we need in order to succeed? (Counsel)
- Exactly what are we going to do short-range, mid-range, and long-range? (Direction)
- Who will be responsible for what? And who will be responsible for whom? (Organization)
- What are our expected expenses and income? (Cash)
- Are we on target? (Reporting)
- How can we effectively make known what we're doing? (Communication)
- Are we seeing the quality we expect or demand from ourselves? (Evaluating)
- How can we keep improving in the critical aspects of this project or service? (Refining)

The masterplanning process will unify your team, clarify your direction and decision making, and increase your leadership confidence.

19 MONEY

Maintaining financial balance is one of the trickiest endeavors in our world. I'm convinced that the key is having the right *perspective* on money—something that isn't easy to get in a money-oriented, spend-more-than-you-make, live-faster-than-you-think, buy-more-than-you-need-or-even-want society.

There are three basic dimensions of making and managing money: (1) generating income, (2) controlling expenses, and (3) managing savings.

It's my impression that a high percentage of Americans generate adequate income. But I believe most of them have trouble in the second area of controlling expenses, and, as a result, are unable to accomplish the critical task of developing adequate savings.

An underlying reason for that, I believe, is the fundamentally different approach to life between people who are financially struggling and those who are financially secure. In the first category, people *live* and then save what's left over; in the second category, they *save* and then live on what's left over.

The following questions will help you develop the kind of perspective that keeps you on top of the financial flow.

Am I generating adequate income?

If you aren't generating enough dollars to pay the bills, you'll soon be bankrupt. It's as simple as that.

Am I controlling expenses so that I have cash reserves?

If you spend all you make, you'll never have a reserve as a cushion and investments that can start making money.

Am I accounting for taxes?

Are you keeping adequate records of how much you made and saved, and how much you spent (and on what) so you know how much tax you really owe?

Do I have a tangible picture—using graphs or charts—of the financial context for future decisions?

A visual account of your financial state is especially necessary in the corporate or organizational setting, but it can be helpful in personal finances as well. Show projected income compared to projected expenses, increases or decreases in actual income, and so on.

When you face a pressing financial decision, ask . . .

From whom should I seek counsel?

On the personal level, what person outside your family can you count on to give you sound financial advice? It should be someone who understands how to generate, save, and manage money properly.

Should I wait to make this decision until I'm more objective about it?

Maybe you're too emotional at the moment—you want something so badly that you're willing to buy when you shouldn't.

Can I afford to lose all this money?

Before you make an investment, ask yourself, "If I lost it all, how would it affect my family, and how would it affect me?"

Exactly why am I making this decision?

Write out your answer, and show it to your financial advisers. Do they agree that it's a good reason?

Is this the right time to take this financial step?

Is this purchase or investment truly at the top of your list? Few people have enough money to buy everything they want or need *when* they want or need it. I keep a "some-day" list of things I'd like to buy; then when I get a few extra dollars, I take out the list and ask, "Which item is the highest priority for the money I now have?"

And finally, I'll pass along this good reminder that a friend of mine often says:

When your outgo
exceeds your income,
your upkeep
will be your downfall!

Remember

To keep your thinking on managing money, ask yourself these fundamental questions:

- Am I generating adequate income?
- Am I controlling expenses so that I have cash reserves?
- Am I accounting for taxes?
- Do I have a tangible picture—using graphs or charts—of the financial context for future decisions?

When you face a pressing financial decision, ask:

- From whom should I seek counsel?
- Should I wait to make this decision until I'm more objective about it?
- Can I afford to lose all this money?
- Exactly *why* am I making this decision?
- Is this the right time to take this financial step?

Knowing the right money questions helps increase your leadership confidence.

MOTIVATING YOURSELF

The fires of motivation are fed by the fuel of dreams. If you're ever down . . . if you ever go through a week or two (or more) when you have to push yourself just to get out of bed, let alone accomplish some great goal . . . if you ever feel you've lost the touch that let you achieve your past successes—then use these questions to revive your motivation.

Do I have clear, meaningful, and achievable goals?

Once again, look at chapter 16 on "Goal Setting," particularly at the Life Focus Chart. When you look at the future, your motivation returns, and so does your discipline (remember that motivation and discipline are two sides of the same coin). If your goals are strong, your motivation is strong; and if your motivation is strong, your discipline is strong.

Few things motivate like success, and success is the feeling you get when you reach your goals. With clear goals you have a clear path to success—and to motivation.

Why am I doing what I'm doing?

Many motivational speakers emphasize the need for being accountable to another person—someone to give you a tap on the shoulder when you aren't doing what you should. This kind of friend can be helpful, but I don't believe an accountability partner is the only source of true motivation. Another source, and an outstanding one, is the "hidden dream" that many people have, a dream of what they would someday most like to do, to be, or to have—a dream that they tell to very few people, if any.

What's your hidden dream? When you're down with discouragement, pull it out and take another look at your dream in the privacy of your mind, and let it begin motivating you.

In what areas of my life am I growing personally?

Stagnation isn't very motivating. If you're feeling stagnant, try learning something new. (However, don't try it yet if you're experiencing fatigue and stress—taking on a new responsibility may only add to your sense of being overwhelmed.) If you're operating on natural energy (see chap. 13) and have clear goals, select a new area for personal growth and it will be a fresh source of motivation.

Personal growth is exponential. The more you learn, the more opportunities you have to learn even more.

Am I fatigued?

The negative introspection associated with fatigue could be robbing you of motivation. (See chap. 14.)

What demotivators can I get rid of?

What demotivators are present in your life today? Here are five common demotivators—are you having to deal with any of them?

- Having to work in an area of personal weakness instead of an area of personal strength.
- Indecision. What are you trying to decide today? What are the three top decisions you need to make in the next two weeks to two months?
- The sense of being overwhelmed. If you could do only three things this week, what would they be? Try completing those.
- Feeling totally blocked in—as if your path was buried by an avalanche—in some area of life.
- The lack of clear goals.

If these primary demotivators are present in your life—how can you remove them?

Is my life focused on giving or getting?

What special gift can you offer someone in the next week? The simple act of giving often brings back a motivated excitement for life.

What needs do I most want to do something about this year?

By clearly seeing the needs of other people—perhaps more deeply than you ever have before—you can regain motivation to meet those needs. Ask yourself, "What needs do I feel deeply concerned about—and uniquely qualified to meet?" Then spend time meeting those specific needs in the immediate future.

Is my career path clearly in view?

You may have set a lot of goals, including many related to your work, and yet not know where they will lead you in terms of your own career. But if you do know where each goal is taking you—if your career path is clear—it unlocks tremendous natural motivation.

What difference am I really making?

Another key question is, "What difference do I want to make?" This is where *significance* enters in, as compared to *success* or *survival.* Focus on the difference you want to make a year or five years from now, and it will give you a progressive sense of encouragement and motivation.

Finally, remember once again to maintain and review a Positive Progress List (see chap. 6). It's like storing a pocketful of sunshine for a rainy day. For the most meaningful encouragement, remember to keep a written record of the lives you've changed.

Remember

In the future, whenever you sense the need to renew your self-motivation, turn to this chapter and ask yourself these questions:

- Do I have clear, meaningful, and achievable goals?
- Why am I doing what I am doing?
- In what areas of my life am I growing personally?
- Am I fatigued?
- What demotivators can I get rid of?
- Is my life focused on giving or getting?
- What needs do I most want to do something about this year?
- Is my career path clearly in view?
- What difference am I really making?

The right questions can restore your excitement for the future and strengthen your leadership confidence.

21 MOTIVATING OTHERS

I don't consider myself a "motivational" speaker, and I don't have a supercharged personality. But people have often said to me, "Bobb, you really motivate me."

At first I almost wanted to apologize because I wasn't intending to "hype" them. Then I began to ask myself: What causes a person to really motivate others, even inadvertently?

I believe the key factor is *having the right assumptions about people.* Perhaps the five most important assumptions I can make about people are these:

- People do what makes sense to them.
- No one really wants to fail.
- Everyone wants to make a difference.
- Everyone wants to grow personally.
- Everyone needs and responds to encouragement.

These are all positive assumptions, the kind of beliefs that ward off negative judgments such as "That's a stupid thing he just did," or "She's always trying to undermine everything," or "He's hopeless," or "It's useless trying to motivate them."

Think of one person whom you would most like to motivate, and ask yourself whether the five assumptions listed above are your genuine beliefs about him or her. Then think through the following questions to help you gain and keep a positive perspective about this person.

What are this person's three greatest strengths?

Anyone working in areas of personal weakness rather than areas of personal strength will not be motivated. To put it another way, if anyone has been grinding away at tasks assigned in their weak areas and you reassign him to work in his strength areas, you'll see a drastic increase in his natural motivation.

Perhaps this person needs help in identifying his key strengths. Help him discover and understand them, and learn to take advantage of them at work, at home, and in all his relationships.

What are this person's three most critical short-term decisions?

What is it that this person needs to decide *on the inside?* What is he or she trying to decide but just can't make a decision?

Discovering these issues can be as simple as asking the person, "What are your three most critical decisions to make in the near future?" Indecisiveness during an intensive time of life always undermines motivation.

What are this person's top three measurable goals for the next month?

If the person is overwhelmed by all the things he has to do, help him define the three most important things to do now. Taking a few simple steps will help him feel in control again.

What are this person's top three measurable goals for the next two years?

In my observation, the greatest single reason for demotivation in people is that they operate in a day-to-day firefighting mode, just trying to survive, and they don't have compelling goals that pull them into the future.

> I have never seen a man who could do real work
> except under the stimulus of
> encouragement and enthusiasm, and the approval
> of the people for whom he is working.
> —*Charles Schwab*

Help this person define even *one* significant, measurable goal for the next two years—something he wants to do, or be, or have. With the clarity that comes from focusing on the future rather than drowning in the present, tremendous motivation can be unlocked.

I believe people are naturally motivated to do incredible things. Most of us can recall a time in our lives when we were overflowing with natural energy. It was easy to get up in the morning and hard to go to bed at night. Then we experienced various demotivators such as indecisiveness, blurry priorities, or a lack of goals, and it began to be difficult to motivate ourselves.

Although these demotivators hold us down, deep within us our motivational motor is still running. The potential is still there, and our desire to succeed and excel is still there.

So help people get rid of their demotivators.

What are the three major obstacles facing this person?

In what areas does this person feel that life has shut him down completely? Is it a lack of education? A lack of money? A lack of brainpower?

Find out the things which he feels must be corrected before life will be right for him. Help him to start unlocking them or to find creative ways around them.

What are the three major resources this person can bring to bear on his situation?

If he feels as if he's trapped within a canyon, help him find the right ladder to climb out.

What are this person's fears?

Do you remember the elephant stakes story at the beginning of this book? Ask yourself: What lingering fears and hang-ups does this person have? And how has his self-perception been limited by wrong conclusions from the past? Help him identify those stakes and pull them up. Help him see that he can do things now that a year ago he couldn't, and that a year from now he'll be able to do even more.

What are this person's dreams?

You may want to help him complete his own copy of the Life Focus Chart in chapter 16.

What could this person do if he or she had access to significantly more resources?

What could he or she do if he had unlimited money and other resources? This is sometimes the kind of question that unlocks your ability to see clearly this person's true potential.

How can I help this person grow personally?

Another way to ask it: What would I want to help this person learn if he or she were my brother or sister, or my mother or father?

Make a lifelong study of the subjects of motivation and demotivation. Everything you learn will be of enduring value as you work with people.

Remember

To stay alert to the best ways to motivate someone, turn to this chapter often, and ask yourself these questions:

- What are this person's three greatest strengths?
- What are this person's three most critical short-term decisions?
- What are this person's top three measurable goals for the next month?
- What are this person's top three measurable goals for the next two years?
- What are the three major obstacles facing this person?
- What are the three major resources this person can bring to bear on his situation?
- What are this person's fears?
- What are this person's dreams?
- What could this person do if he or she had access to significantly more resources?
- How can I help this person grow personally?

The right questions will help you over a lifetime to develop the critical skill of motivating others, thus increasing your leadership confidence.

22 PEOPLE BUILDING

The greatest satisfaction in leadership—the feeling of accomplishment that means the most when you look back on it after ten or twenty or fifty years—is the satisfaction of *building people.*

Satisfaction is the feeling that comes from achieving *quality*—not only in products or services, but also in relationships. You can *use* people to accomplish your goals, but the feeling of satisfaction will be nothing compared to the deep fulfillment that comes from building up people *as* you accomplish your goals.

The ideal approach to life is this: *Love everyone unconditionally.* As you progress toward this ideal, you'll be a stronger person and a stronger leader, and far more satisfied. It's the foundational philosophy in people building.

Are you truly building up the people who work for you, as well as others whose lives you influence?

Use these questions to help you decide.

Do I know how to love unconditionally?

Unconditional love means your love and concern for a person goes on regardless of what they do or don't do. It means treating your staff in the way you want your own family members to be treated.

Do I really believe that . . .

- no one wants to fail?
- people do what makes sense to *them?*
- people who seem lazy really aren't (they simply haven't been properly motivated)?
- everyone wants to grow personally?
- everyone wants to make an important difference?

I've found in life that all five of those statements are very, very accurate. Reflect on them, and I think you'll also conclude they're true.

Do I encourage, appreciate, affirm, and recognize people?

- *Encouragement* means giving hope for the future—"You're going to make it!"
- *Appreciation* is simply saying thank you—"Thanks for helping out," "Thanks for staying late," "I really appreciate how you've gone out of your way to help the team on this."
- *Affirmation* is expressing your admiration for someone's personal strengths—"You're a very caring per-

son," "I really respect your honesty," or "You're very skilled at public speaking."

- *Recognition* is expressing your awareness of someone's accomplishments—"You did a great job on that report," or "You've really put together a great team."

Learn to excel in these facets of relating to everyone—family, friends, and staff. Few other strengths are more important to a leader of people.

And give your encouragement to other leaders as well. Most leaders need encouragement far more than they need criticism.

> People want to be appreciated, not impressed.
> They want to be regarded as human beings,
> not as sounding boards for other people's egos.
> They want to be treated as an end in themselves, not
> as a means toward the gratification of another's vanity.
> —*Sydney J. Harris*

Am I truly building people—or merely building my own dream and using people to do it?

Ask yourself, "Am I just using this person to get the job done, or do I see this as an opportunity to build into his life?"

Do I care enough to confront people when they really need it?

Is someone doing something that is harmful to himself as well as to the rest of the team? Could it handicap him for the rest of his life if he doesn't learn how to be more disciplined, more honest, more neat in his appearance, or whatever? Are you willing to do it for the person's benefit as well as yours and the team's?

> Every person deserves to know clearly how his manager feels about his performance.

Confrontation is very difficult for most people. If you feel uneasy just reading the word *confront,* I'd suggest that you substitute the word *clarify.* Clarify the issues instead of confronting the person.

Am I listening to people with more than my ears? Am I hearing more than their words?

Am I listening to the *emotional* content of what others say, as well as to their words? What is *not* being said? What are they feeling, but not expressing in words? What can you tell from their actions and gestures?

If an outsider came in to watch your team communicate, what would he see that you don't? If another firm's recruiter came in to evaluate these people, what strengths would he see in them? What have you been overlooking?

Are you sensitive, or are you pressing ahead so hard that you don't listen? Do you recognize and try to meet each person's needs for appreciation and understanding?

Do I round out the "flat sides" of my staff?

How can you help staff members deal with situations that are holding them back or areas of weakness that are keeping them from becoming well-rounded leaders? What are those flat sides, and how can you help your staff develop them so that, a year from now, they'll be far stronger than they are now?

Am I helping my staff members develop their greatest strengths?

What do you see as the greatest single strength in each of your staff members? Let them know what you see, and ask each one, "How can I help you build up this strength?" Build on each other's strengths.

Do I understand the true long-term potential of each of my staff members?

Imagine each of your staff members twenty years from now. What potential does each one have? How can you help each one grow into that full potential?

> The greatest good you can do for another is not just to share your riches, but to reveal to him his own.
> —*Benjamin Disraeli*

Do my staff members know I want them to reach their fullest personal potential?

Beginning on the previous page is a list of questions to ask in a "building" interview—a once-a-year, one-to-one communication session in which you let your staff members tell you individually how they would like to improve

Questions to Ask (as appropriate) in Annual "Building" Interviews with Your Staff

- What is the most meaningful thing you have experienced in the last year?
- Where do you really want to grow personally this year—and how can I help you grow in these areas?
- What are you planning to do this year that you have never done before? And what, if any, anxiety do you feel about it?
- What courses would you like to take—what books would you like to read—what experiences would you like to have to help you grow this year?
- What is the most helpful thing for me to know about you, to truly understand "the real you"?
- What are your dreams for the next five to ten years?
- What do you consider your three greatest strengths, and how can I help you maximize them?
- What do you feel is holding you back in any aspect of your life—and how can I help you overcome it?
- What is the single area of your life that you would most like me to encourage you in this year?
- In what aspect of your work do you find the most personal fulfillment—and why?
- What areas of your work cause you the most personal stress and frustration—and why?
- What tools, equipment, facilities, or personnel could help you most in maximizing your potential on the job?
- In what area would you like to see me grow this year? Is this an area that you feel you could help in, or suggest someone who could?

continued

- What do I do that demotivates you?
- What do I do that motivates you?
- Is there any unresolved problem that you have been hoping to speak to me about but haven't known how to approach the subject?
- Is there anything heavy on your shoulders (outside of work) that you would like to talk with me about as a friend?

in the coming year, and how you can help. Give them a copy of the questions, have them think about them for a week and record their answers, then meet with them over lunch to talk about it. This process lets them know you care personally about them and sensitizes you to the ways they want to grow.

Finally, do I know what position each of my staff members would like to attain in the next five years? And am I helping each one to grow into it?

Remember

To keep sharpening your people-building skills, turn frequently to this chapter and ask yourself these questions:

- Do I know how to love unconditionally?
- Do I really believe that
  —no one wants to fail?
  —people do what makes sense to them?
  —people who seem lazy really aren't (they simply haven't been properly motivated)?
  —everyone wants to grow personally?
  —everyone wants to make an important difference?
- Do I encourage, appreciate, affirm, and recognize people?
- Am I truly building people—or merely building my own dream and using people to do it?
- Do I care enough to confront people when they really need it?
- Am I listening to people with more than my ears—am I hearing more than their words?
- Do I round out the "flat sides" of my staff?
- Am I helping my staff members develop their greatest strengths?
- Do I understand the true long-term potential of each of my staff members?
- Do my staff members know I want them to reach their fullest personal potential?
- Do I know what position each of my staff members would like to attain in the next five years? And am I helping each one to grow into it?

As you grow in your ability to build up others, you'll be strengthening one of the most crucial components of your leadership confidence.

23 PERSONAL ORGANIZATION

It was written in glittering letters on a five-by-seven-inch cardboard plaque that hung on my grandmother's wall: "A Place for Everything and Everything in Its Place."

Years later, as I was exploring the subject of personal organization for senior executives, thinking through critical factors and various sophisticated theories, it dawned on me that the old adage quoted on my grandmother's wall represented the essence of what I was searching for. It's the essence of personal organization.

If you feel as personally organized as you'd like to feel, you can skip to the next chapter and make a mental note to come back to these pages whenever that sense of order starts to slacken.

But if you're ready now to bring more organization to your life—the following questions can help.

Do I have a to-do list that works for me?

Your to-do list may be on computer, in a sophisticated notebook with dozens of category dividers, or on a three-by-five card that you carry in your shirt pocket—whatever works for you is fine. But each of us needs a place to write down the things we're committed to doing. Otherwise, as our responsibilities increase and our level of leadership grows, more and more important things will drop through the cracks.

> Systems—from to-do lists and calendars to libraries and computers—are your servants. They help you do things better and quicker, and by improving them you decrease your time expense and increase your results. So don't fight systems; improve them.

Do I have a calendar that works for me?

Your calendar may also be unlike anyone else's, but the critical point is to have one that *works for you.*

A business or professional person who typically has several short appointments each day probably needs a daily calendar marked off in half-hourly or even quarter-hourly increments.

A calendar lets you keep track of critical planning dates in the future. These important calendar notes become milestones that give you a sense of progress and organization as you pass them.

Do I have quick access to addresses and phone numbers?

As I emphasized earlier, leadership is knowing what to do next, knowing why that's important, and knowing how to bring appropriate resources to bear on the need at hand. Getting in touch with those appropriate resources is a critical reason for having instant access to important addresses and phone numbers.

Do I have a filing system that works for me?

My philosophy on filing systems is "the simpler the better." In my personal system, everything is simply filed alphabetically. For my work, I have a four-level filing system. In my desk is a current projects file. In a separate file drawer near my desk are my client files. In a four-drawer file cabinet just outside my office are project and people files, which typically I won't refer to this week, but probably will sometime in the next year. I also have a "morgue" file for information such as old income tax records—things I don't want to throw away yet, but which I seldom if ever need. Again, whatever *works for you* is the aim.

Almost everything I've learned about personal organization in the past twenty years could be summarized in the topics of those four questions above: having a to-do list that works for you, a calendar that works for you, an address and phone number list that works for you, and a filing system that works for you. Every leader I've met who doesn't have these four things in place is suffering from the negative consequences.

If you don't have them in place for yourself, it's almost certain you will miss an important appointment or deadline, or be unable to find important resources or information when you need them.

Once you have those four systems nailed down, you can go on to develop other helpful aspects of personal organization:

Do I have a "Positive Progress List"?

It's helpful to take an organized look at your personal milestones in the past. Read more about this list in chapter 6 on "Confidence."

Do I regularly set aside time on my calendar for personal organization? And do I keep these appointments with myself?

Set aside time regularly to keep yourself organized—to update your to-do list, to throw away old files, and so on. Otherwise you'll feel trapped in a blizzard of disorganization. Besides the regular, more frequent times, you may also want to spend one day a year reevaluating your systems and doing any needed major reorganization.

What three tools could help make me more effective?

Perhaps a personal computer, a dictation unit, or a state-of-the-art calculator would increase your effectiveness.

John W. Patterson, the man who built the National Cash Register Company, had this philosophy: "Anything a man *needs* in his business, he is paying for—whether he has it or not." If you don't have the right tools, you're paying for them anyway through inefficiency, lost business, or lost time.

Do I have a "Future File"?

In a "Future File" you can keep notes and other material for the future—ideas for books or articles you want to write, plans for an office or home you want to build, or whatever.

I find it especially helpful to get out this file and look through it whenever I'm tempted to get discouraged with the present. It's exciting and motivating to think about tomorrow, and it's good to see progress toward achieving those future dreams.

Finally, remember Peter Drucker's definitions of *efficiency* (doing things right) versus *effectiveness* (doing the right things). As you spend time on personal organization, make sure to keep your focus on *doing the right things*—doing what's truly important.

The more you focus on this *long-term* effectiveness, the more you need simple, practical systems to help you achieve it. In fact, focusing on long-term effectiveness *forces* us to a systematic approach.

A rule of thumb for organizing your overall work strategy:

Work where you're strongest
80 percent of the time.

Work where you're learning
15 percent of the time.

Work where you're weak
5 percent of the time.

Focus on results, *not* activity.

Remember

Whenever you begin to feel disorganized, turn immediately to this chapter, and let these questions help you:

- Do I have a to-do list that works for me?
- Do I have a calendar that works for me?
- Do I have quick access to addresses and phone numbers?
- Do I have a filing system that works for me?
- Do I have a "Positive Progress List"?
- Do I regularly set aside time on my calendar for personal organization? And do I keep these appointments with myself?
- What three tools could help make me more effective?
- Do I have a "Future File"?

Knowing the right questions will help you stay organized—and make possible your leadership confidence.

24 PRESSURE

Pressure must be the most commonly used word in today's English language.

That's an overstatement, but it's probably not too far from being accurate. With all the complexities and changes that keep America on the move, pressure is the unavoidable result.

Pressure means basically the effect of "pressing in"—too many responsibilities, expectations that are too high, deadlines that are too soon. Internally, it can also mean "pressing out"—our overwhelming desires to do, to express, to experience, to accomplish.

I've observed that feeling extreme pressure usually has multiple causes, rather than coming from one dominant source. Rather than feeling they have one giant boulder on their shoulders, people feel they have a pile of rocks, a number of things that are behind schedule or out of balance or needing immediate attention. The cumulative effect is that they feel suffocated.

When the pressure becomes excessive, the best way to keep yourself from bursting like an overinflated balloon is to release the pressure slowly, little by little—taking care of one thing at a time.

If you're feeling major stress today, and you yearn to start the process of releasing the pressure points one by one, let these questions help you.

What specific things are weighing heavily on my shoulders today?

As we've suggested before, make a list of *everything*—big, medium, and small—that's pressuring you. Dump it out of your brain and onto paper. The order of the items doesn't matter.

Your list may have fifty or more items. Which of them can you delay or eliminate entirely? Which are the top three to work on first, taking them one step at a time?

This process alone can help you relieve much of the pressure.

What three decisions are the most pressing today?

After you identify these three decisions, take them through the questioning process presented in chapter 8 on "Decision Making."

Indecision is one of the strongest and most common sources of pressure. The stress level can be excruciating when your responsibility builds while important

Are You Feeling Time Pressure?

Six Perspectives on Time

1 Year

In a new situation, one of the things that causes time pressure is the fact that you don't have a track record. You've never done what you're setting out to do, so you tend to set unrealistically high goals. As Dr. Ted Engstrom says, "A man tends to overestimate what he can do in one year and underestimate what he can do in five."

Try to set low goals for the first year in a new assignment until you build a track record that allows you to increase them.

3 Years

I've talked to many managers who agree that it typically takes three years to get a major new project running smoothly—so that it's truly "going your way."

The first year tends to be a year of orientation and experimentation. You get a feel for the key people, the key variables, the major roadblocks, and so on.

In the second year you launch into what you think are key solutions. You're prototyping what you think will work and revising it.

Often, about halfway into the third year, you experience a sudden feeling that "this will never work," as various difficulties remain to be ironed out. But that feeling usually passes as you continue to make progress.

After three years, either the project will start to be clearly successful, or else it will never be successful.

5 Years

Look again at Ted Engstrom's quote, "A man tends to overestimate what he can do in one year, and underestimate what he can do in five." In most projects, at the end of five years you'll see more than you would have imagined when you started.

10 Years

Plan your life so that ten years from today you'll be at your peak in life. You'll look the best, feel the best, and be more effective than you've ever been. Count on it being the best year of your life.

But every year on your birthday, move that peak year one year later. That way, when you're forty you'll be preparing for the big year at age fifty; when you're fifty, you'll be getting ready for sixty, and so on.

This helps you be a lifelong learner. You'll never reach the point of feeling you've "arrived." You'll always have a future orientation, rather than feeling as if your peak was in the past.

30 Years

How far have you come in the past thirty years? If you continue to be a growing person, your maturity and strengths thirty years in the future will be just as incomprehensible to you now as your present life was thirty years ago. Expect to be surprised.

500 Years

Someday, the ordinary pressures of time you now feel every moment will no longer exist. After time for you has ceased, what legacy will you have left behind?

decisions are delayed. *Make* those decisions, and the stress level will ease.

Am I getting proper rest?

Are you fatigued? If so, find help through the questions in chapter 13.

If I'm overcommitted, how did it happen?

Why am I running so fast? What am I trying to do or be? Am I trying to be rich or famous (or both)? What's the reason, and what difference does it make?

Have I set unrealistically high goals for myself?

Are you pursuing goals that are too demanding? It's healthy to have goals that motivate you, but they shouldn't *master* you.

Am I trying to be perfect?

You don't have to be perfect, and you can't be. So relax.

Who can help me relieve this pressure?

Maybe you need an objective outsider (or insider) to help you see where the pressure is coming from and how to relieve it. Find someone with whom you can talk about it.

Can money help relieve this pressure?

Money can sometimes solve the problems that are causing pressure. Is that the case with you now?

Remember

In the future, whenever you start feeling intense pressure, get out this book, turn to this chapter, and ask yourself these clarifying questions:

- What specific things are weighing heavily on my shoulders today?
- What three decisions are the most pressing today?
- Am I getting proper rest?
- If I'm overcommitted, how did happen?
- Have I set unrealistically high goals for myself?
- Am I trying to be perfect?
- Who can help me relieve this pressure?
- Can money help relieve this pressure?

Knowing the right questions can help eliminate unnecessary pressure and increase your leadership confidence.

25 PRIORITIZING

"I'm going in a thousand different directions. I've got to stop and get my priorities straight." How many times have you felt that way?

Setting right priorities means simply this: deciding what to do next in order to move effectively toward your goals.

> He is a wise man who wastes no energy on pursuits for which he is not fitted; and he is wiser still who from among the things he can do well, chooses and resolutely follows the best.
>
> —*William Gladstone*

Most people don't effectively prioritize because they don't have goals. *Without goals, setting appropriate priorities is impossible.* Of course, goal setting itself involves prioritizing. By choosing a goal while ignoring or rejecting others, you're saying, "*This* is a more important thing to do than *that*."

As the Italian economist Pereto suggests, if you were Noah, and the ark was beginning to sink, you would throw off the elephants first. Setting right priorities is like that. You identify the actions that will have the most significant and beneficial impact, and you do those first.

> Prioritizing is simply deciding what you need to do next to move most effectively toward your goals.

Let these questions help you set right priorities:

If I could achieve only three measurable goals this year, what would they be?

This is a real fog-lifter. The things you would do if they were all you could do—in the next year, the next five, or for your whole life—these are your *priorities.*

To help you in this thinking process, the special list of questions on page 184 can be looked at once a year.

> Besides the noble art of getting things done, there is the noble art of leaving things undone. The wisdom of life consists of the elimination of nonessentials.
> —*Lin Yutang*
>
> Deciding what *not* to do is just as important as deciding what to do.
> —*Archie B. Parrish*

What are the top six things I want to accomplish in the next three months?

Make a list. It's important to have this kind of intermediate goals, which serve as priorities in moving you toward your one-year goals.

If I could choose only three things to get done today, what would they be?

These are the immediate goals that will move you toward your intermediate goals and annual goals.

What are all the things I need to accomplish in the next seven days? And how would I rate their importance?

As we've suggested before, this is an exhaustive list of the things you need or want to do—whether twenty items, fifty, or seventy-five.

When the list is complete, assign a priority level to each item. Give the most important things an *A,* everything on the next level a *B,* and less important items a *C* or *D.* Then go through all the A-level items, and number them in priority order: Al, A2, A3, etc.

> I soon learned to scent out that which was able to lead to fundamentals and to turn aside everything else, from the multitude of things that clutter up the mind and divert it from the essential.
>
> —*Albert Einstein*

A Single Year

(Questions to ask yourself once a year,
on your birthday, or each New Year's Day)

- What is my single greatest strength or uniqueness as a person?
- What single need or situation do I feel most deeply burdened by and uniquely qualified to meet?
- What single person would I most like to build up, develop, or teach this year?
- What single person would I most like to learn from this year?
- What single thing would I do this year if it was all I could do?
- What single thing would I most like to buy this year?
- What single place would I most like to visit this year?
- What is the greatest single roadblock holding me back this year?
- What single thing would be the most helpful in removing that roadblock?
- What single question or problem would I give ten percent of my personal income to have answered or solved this year?
- What single principle or truth would I most like to teach a group of people this year?
- What single habit would I most like to break this year?
- What single habit would I most like to establish this year?
- What single area of my entire life would I most like to grow in personally this year?

Typically, I can go through my average to-do list of about thirty-five items and prioritize them in this fashion in about two minutes.

What items on my to-do list am I truly committed to doing? And what items are only things I would like to get done but am not committed to?

Again, you have to distinguish between what you truly need to do and what you only want to do.

What things on my list can be delegated to someone else?

Look at chapter 9 on "Delegating" for help on this.

What things on my list can be postponed?

Even postponing something a week often relieves pressure and helps you reprioritize quickly.

What things on my list can I safely decide not to do at all?

Remember, deciding what *not* to do is critical.

Do I need a friend to help me look objectively at my priorities?

Who could this be for you?

Distinguish between . . .

what is a good use of your money from what is the best use
what is a good use of your time from what is the best use
what is a good use of your energy from what is the best use

Remember

In the future, when you need help in better choosing what to do next to meet your goals, turn to this chapter and ask these questions:

- If I could achieve only three measurable goals this year, what would they be?
- What are the top six things I want to accomplish in the next three months?
- If I could choose only three things to accomplish today, what would they be?
- What are all the things I need to accomplish in the next seven days? And how would I rate their importance?
- What items on my to-do list am I truly committed to doing? And what items are only things I would like to get done but am not committed to?
- What things on my list can be delegated to someone else?
- What things on my list can be postponed?
- What things on my list can I safely decide not to do at all?
- Do I need a friend to help me look objectively at my priorities?

Knowing the right questions will make you wiser in choosing priorities and will increase your leadership confidence.

26 PROBLEM SOLVING

Solving a problem doesn't end our problems—it simply brings up the next one.

Every human being has to cope with problems all the time, and that's why there is lifelong value in mastering the questions below. They won't eliminate problems from your life, but they do present a *process* for dealing with them effectively.

How would I prioritize the problems I face today?

Richard Sloma says, "Never try to solve all the problems all at once—make them line up for you one-by-one." Whether you face three problems, thirty, or three hundred, make them stand in single file so you face only one at a time.

In a single sentence, what is the problem?

Keep in mind the difference between *solving a problem* and *decision making.* A decision is a choice you make between two or more alternatives: "Should I fly to Phoenix or Chicago?" A problem is a situation that's counter to your intentions or expectations: "I meant to fly to Chicago, but I ended up in Detroit." Or, "I meant to have $50,000 in the bank, but I'm $50,000 in the hole."

How is my personal balance or imbalance affecting my ability to solve this problem?

Are you emotionally or physically fatigued? If so, it may take you hours of struggle to find a solution that you might otherwise discover in minutes.

What are the facts related to this problem?

Remember Peter Drucker's words: "Once the facts are clear, the decisions jump out at you." What are the facts related to the problem? What are your most realistic options for solving it?

Why does the problem exist?

What caused this problem, and how can we keep it from ever happening again?

What are the three greatest resources I can bring to bear on this problem?

The best resources might be other people, formulas, tools, or something else. Write them down.

Who can help me solve this problem?

An expert—someone who really knows this field in a deep way—might be able to help you. Or perhaps simply finding someone with an objective viewpoint could help, someone who sees the situation differently from those involved in it day to day.

Should I spend more money to reduce the time needed to solve this problem?

If you have the money, you can typically buy the tools or hire the people to help shorten the amount of time it will take to find a solution.

Some problems are so critical they must be solved immediately, and thus require lots of money to solve—for example, an oil refinery fire that is burning off countless gallons of fuel each minute. Other problems can wait.

And, of course, some problems take a certain amount of time regardless of the amount of resources you spend. For example, to make a baby takes nine months, regardless of the number of mothers you assign to the task.

Of all the potential solutions to this problem, which one has the greatest potential to be right? And which one involves the lowest risk?

Weigh *all* the possible solutions before deciding, then go to the single best solution.

What policy would keep this problem from recurring?

Few people can give a clear definition for the word *policy.* A working definition for a leader's purpose is this: *A policy is something we always do, or something we never do.*

In the process of solving the problem, learn what you can to help you avoid a recurrence.

Remember

Whenever you struggle with a major problem, get out this book, turn to this chapter, and ask yourself these questions:

- How would I prioritize the problems I face today?
- In a single sentence, what is the problem?
- How is my personal balance or imbalance affecting my ability to solve this problem?
- What are the facts related to this problem?
- Why does the problem exist?
- What are the three greatest resources I can bring to bear on this problem?
- Who can help me solve this problem?
- Should I spend more money to reduce the time needed to solve this problem?
- Of all the potential solutions to this problem, which one has the greatest potential to be right? And which one involves the lowest risk?
- What policy would keep this problem from recurring?

Knowing and asking the right questions leads to the right solutions and helps increase your leadership confidence.

27 RECRUITING

From 60 to 80 percent of the success of any company or organization is attributable to three factors: (1) having a clear direction, (2) having the right team of players, and (3) having sound finances. That's why few things are as important as putting the right people in the right positions.

How do we do that?

Half the job of successful recruiting is simply *knowing what you want done.* Once you know that, and after you have a candidate for the job, the other half of successful recruiting is knowing what *he or she wants done.* If those two things are the same, you have the beginning of a great working relationship.

When hiring a personal assistant, I usually want someone who (a) is a skilled editor, (b) is an excellent typist, (c) is comfortable and gifted in relating with people, (d) enjoys answering the telephone and making calls, and (e) is good at making trip arrangements. If I ask someone in a job interview, "What do you really enjoy doing?" and that person's list includes those five things, I begin to get excited about the possible match.

Let's look at the questions that can help us make better matches.

Exactly what is the job that needs to be done?

On paper, define the position in as much detail as possible, and list the needed strengths and skills that a person in this position needs. *Know what you want done.*

How much can and will I pay for this position?

Make sure you have the resources both to hire the right person and to allow him or her to do the job.

When a strong candidate is under consideration, ask:

Have I checked the right references?

Ask about the candidate's honesty. If you can't trust someone at every point, including the little things, then you really can't trust him at all.

Second, ask also about the candidate's teachability. If he isn't teachable, he's stopped growing.

Should this person be given tests or inventories?

Preliminary testing, such as an inventory of a person's role preferences or personality traits, can be helpful in giving you a better picture of the candidate—how he or she thinks and feels and relates to other people.

The purpose of this kind of evaluation is not to determine a final decision, but to uncover any questions that may need to be explored further before making a final decision.

Would I want someone I love to work for this person? Why or why not?

Would you want your child or spouse or some other family member to work for this candidate? If not, you don't want that person on your staff, leading and influencing others.

What lingering questions do I have about this person?

Answer at least 99 percent of these before making a final hiring decision. Answer any doubts in your mind.

I encourage you to conduct at least two or three interviews with the person. Questions almost always come to mind later after a first interview—questions that are better to answer in a second interview rather than after you've hired the person.

It's helpful also to give the candidate a sample work assignment after the first interview. If possible, a trial period in the position would be ideal, both for the employer and the employee.

If I feel confident this person can do the job, why do I feel that way?

During the interviewing process, describe in detail a tough work situation that he or she might possibly encounter after being hired, and ask, "What would you do if that happened?"

At this point there's no hiding behind a résumé. The candidate either knows how to respond well or doesn't know.

Am I in favor of hiring this person because of his or her obvious strengths or because of a lack of any glaring weaknesses?

What are the primary strengths you are looking for in someone to fill the position—and does this candidate have them?

What else should I ask this person before making a final hiring decision?

Again, get your lingering questions out on the table. Check out anything questionable that came up as you spoke with references.

Once a hiring decision has been made, what assumptions have I made that need to be spelled out in writing?

As Jerry Ballard says, "All miscommunications are the result of differing assumptions." Do you and the new staff member agree exactly about what he or she will be doing, how much the pay will be, and other important aspects?

REMEMBER

Each time you prepare to hire a new staff member, turn to this chapter and ask yourself these questions:

- Exactly what is the job that needs to be done?
- How much can and will I pay for this position?

When a strong candidate is under consideration, ask:

- Have I checked the right references?
- Should this person be given tests or inventories?
- Would I want someone I love to work for this person? Why or why not?
- What lingering questions do I have about this person?
- If I feel confident this person can do the job, why do I feel that way?
- Am I In favor of hiring this person because of his or her obvious strengths or because of a lack of any glaring weaknesses?
- What else should I ask this person before making a final hiring decision?
- Once a hiring decision has been made, what assumptions have I made that need to be spelled out in writing?

Knowing the right questions will sharpen and objectify your hiring skills, and will help increase your leadership confidence.

28 REPORTING

As a leader, you are responsible for helping your staff achieve *their* goals—goals which you and they have agreed on.

To help them do that, you are responsible to serve your staff in at least these five ways:

- Give them clear-cut decisions when needed.
- Help them make realistic, well-defined, achievable goals and plans.
- Help them remove obstacles that keep them from reaching their goals.
- Encourage them as they achieve key milestones.
- Be aware of personal issues in their lives so you can stand by them when they're feeling low and celebrate with them when they're on top of the world.

Of course, you can't accomplish this list if you don't know what decisions they need, what problems they're having, what goals they're setting, and what progress they're making.

That's where *reporting* comes in.

Effective reporting from your staff assumes that each staff member has clearly stated goals that the two of you have agreed to. Without these goals, there is really no reason for your staff to report to you. I can't underscore that enough.

Once the goals are in place, your interest in the process of reporting is based on your commitment to help your staff achieve their goals.

The questions below are for your use in getting the information you need from your staff.

You can also adapt them for your use in reporting to your manager or board. These questions will help you determine what ground you need to cover as you communicate with them, and what you need to ask them.

What *decisions* do you need from me?

Even top-level executive staff members will seldom move out ahead of you in a situation in which they need a clear, major decision from you. They will *wait* for that decision, and sometimes that means feeling "blocked in" and unable to move forward. If you don't give them that decision, they can hardly be held responsible for not reaching their goals on time.

On a regular basis, find out what decisions they need from you. In their regular written reports to you, staff members should state these clearly.

What *problems* are you facing on which my input is needed?

Usually your staff should have only two or three problems that they need your help on. If they come up with twenty or thirty, it probably means you are not having reporting sessions often enough, or some of the problems are too small and could actually be handled efficiently without your input.

When they report a problem, they should also present three possible solutions for it, along with a recommended option. If a staff member tells you, "The new computer program isn't working," he should also be able to say something like, "I see our three options as (1) getting a new computer, (2) reprogramming the one we have, or (3) having an expert come in to take a look. I recommend option three, because . . . ."

Instead of arriving at that same conclusion after a discussion that takes up your time, now you can say simply, "I agree. Go ahead." Always have your staff come to you with their homework done.

What *plans* are you making that we have not discussed?

Sometimes staff members will be pursuing solutions or projects that are more costly than you can afford. You want to know about them before the money is committed.

More about Reporting

Answers to Your Questions

How often should I have the staff report?
Weekly, biweekly, and monthly reports are common. The more complicated and nonroutine the job, the more you will want to meet to keep abreast of progress and problems.

Should reports always be written?
Written reports are my recommendation for full-time staff.

What if a staff member fails to submit a report?
Talk to him, and explain the importance of reporting in allowing you to provide help. If you don't know what he's doing, you can't help him.

If I introduce a reporting system, what reaction can I expect from the staff?
Typically, a breakdown like this:

From 80 percent—relief and appreciation for your commitment to staff.

From 15 percent—fear, because of a lack of confidence in their performance.

From 5 percent—resistance, typically from a distaste for "authority."

How should staff meetings fit into the reporting system?
Some of the reporting questions presented in this chapter are better discussed in a one-to-one setting—such as "What decisions do you need from me?" "What problems are you facing on which my input is needed?" and "How are you doing personally?" Others are more appropriate for a group session: "What plans are you making that we have not discussed?" and "What progress have you made?"

What *progress* have you made?

If you know this, you can encourage them.

How are you doing *personally*?

Again, by knowing this you'll be able to offer needed encouragement at the right time.

Other questions:

Are each staff member's top three annual goals clearly understood?

How frequently is a report needed from each staff member?

What visuals—graphs and charts, etc.—need to be regularly presented and updated by staff members?

What information from my staff do I need to pass on to my manager or board?

A Sample Staff Report Form

Name: ______________________________________

Date: ______________________________________

I need a *decision* from you on the following items:

I am having a *problem* with the following:

I am *planning* to:

I have made *progress* in the following areas:

Here's an update on how I'm doing *personally:*

Remember

To establish and maintain a reporting system that helps you help your staff to meet their goals, review these questions:

Questions for Your Staff

- What *decisions* do you need from me?
- What *problems* are you facing on which my input is needed?
- What *plans* are you making that we have not discussed?
- What *progress* have you made?
- How are you doing *personally?*

Questions for You:

- Are each staff member's top three annual goals clearly understood?
- How frequently is a report needed from each staff member?
- What visuals—graphs and charts, etc.—need to be regularly presented and updated by staff members?
- What information from my staff do I need to pass on to my manager or board?

Knowing and asking the right questions will help you truly support your staff and increase your leadership confidence.

29 RISK TAKING

"Until you know the *worst* that could possibly happen and the *best* that could possibly happen, your equation is incomplete."

Those words from Paul Shultheis (a corporate president and my longtime friend) capture the essence of wise risk taking.

When taking a risk is mentioned, some people's knee-jerk reaction is to say, "It won't work—here's what will go wrong. . . ." They're always looking on the down side. Others are what I call "blue-sky people." They constantly have a wonderful idea in view and seldom think about what could go wrong with it. They don't even see the risk.

Maturity comes in looking at both sides and then making a wise decision. It's weighing the evidence and then saying, "Yes it could go wrong, and yes it could go right; but here's where we are—and we're ready [or not ready] to take this risk."

> **Planning and Risks**
>
> Only rarely are business failures or poor decisions the result of too much planning; almost universally they can be traced to management ego—the temptation to say "I don't need a plan; I'm sure I can handle whatever develops."
>
> —*Richard S. Sloma*

What major risk are you considering today? A major purchase? A big move? A new business? Whatever it is, let these questions help you analyze it and arrive at a wise decision.

What's the worst thing that could happen?

If you tend to be an optimist, ask a pessimist to take a look at the situation with you.

What's the best thing that could happen?

If you tend to be a pessimist, ask an optimist to take a look at the situation with you.

Is it worth the risk?

After asking those first two questions, you've reached the fundamental issue: *Is it worth the risk?*

Actually, every decision you make contains an element of risk. As a leader, you can't avoid taking risks. But you can avoid foolish risks.

Have I sought proper counsel?

If it's a major risk of money, have a trusted financial adviser take a look at it. If it involves the possibility of a major legal liability, have an attorney look at it with you. Whatever risk you're considering, find someone who has experience in that area, preferably someone who has taken a similar risk several times.

Do I fully understand the process and context of the situation?

Are you making the decision on facts (what you *know* to be true) or on assumptions (what you only *believe* to be true)?

Lay out every step and aspect of the proposed plan or project or purchase, and analyze them carefully. Find out what you need to know to turn your assumptions into facts.

Have I asked the key Mind-Stretcher Questions?

Again, look at these questions in chapter 1 to stimulate your best thinking.

Have I established definite criteria for any risk I take?

In other words, what are the conditions under which you have determined you will take any risk?

How can I break down the project or task into sequential steps in order to minimize risk, yet still keep it going?

Dr. Ted Engstrom, president emeritus of World Vision, recommends "buying short" (buying less than you project you'll need) when purchasing for a new project: "It's better to pay a little more up front than to end up with a warehouse full of unneeded materials."

Have I established test milestones: go/no-go points?

Set up the proposed project in phases, and build in go/no-go points at which you can reevaluate whether it's realistic to proceed before investing more resources.

What risks am I taking by *not* acting in the situation?

For example: Maybe you'll never be able to get the needed property at this price again.

What research could check my assumptions about the risk?

Don't proceed in the belief that "the public will love this new project" when a quick check with any ten people on the street could tell you otherwise.

Am I in agreement with the team about our basic assumptions regarding this risk?

Avoid team disagreements that could be costly at some later, more critical point.

Everyone must take risks. But planning and research—and asking the right questions—can help reduce the number of unnecessary and unwise risks you take.

Remember

In the future, whenever you're considering a major risk, get out this book, turn to this chapter, and ask yourself these fundamental questions:

- What's the worst thing that could happen?
- What's the best thing that could happen?
- Is it worth the risk?
- Have I sought proper counsel?
- Do I fully understand the process and context of the situation?
- Have I asked the key Mind-Stretcher Questions?
- Have I established definite criteria for any risk I take?
- How can I break down the project or task into sequential steps in order to minimize risk, yet still keep it going?
- Have I established test milestones: go/no-go points?
- What risks am I taking by *not* acting in the situation?
- What research could check my assumptions about the risk?
- Am I in agreement with the team about our basic assumptions regarding this risk?

Knowing and asking the right questions can make you a more mature risk taker and increase your leadership confidence.

30 TEAM BUILDING

A lot of people think of team building as just so much Rah!-Rah!—getting everyone hyped up through pep talks.

But to develop a team of people united in a sustained commitment to a common purpose is more complicated than that. It takes more planning and effort than a go-for-it speech at halftime.

Here are a few questions to help you focus on the more substantial components of team building.

What is our team's inspirational dream?

People need a dream—and a dream, as you'll remember from chapter 12, is simply what would happen if a need were met—a need that you deeply long to meet. It's the goal of seeing that need fulfilled.

Imagine being on a professional football team whose only goal was to practice. They had no thoughts of winning a division championship or the Super Bowl.

Obviously, it's going for a goal—a dream—that makes being on a team worthwhile.

What is your team's dream? What do you want to someday accomplish together?

> Constant encouragement is like oil or grease in the gears of team "machinery."

What is our practical masterplan?

Is everyone on the team aware of your masterplan? Are your plans laid out in such a way that, as you pass milestones and reach goals, the team shares in the excitement?

Masterplanning is like harnessing ten powerful horses to a single plow—it coordinates all that energy and potential to a single task, moving in a single direction. (See chap. 18 to review masterplanning.)

What training and tools do we need individually and as a team?

You'll be eager to provide the right training and tools as you commit yourself to building up the men and women on your team. In the process of getting the job done, build up the players as well. You can do both! And giving your staff the right training and tools is a big part of it.

What communications system do we need to keep the team on one track?

Look again at chapter 28 on "Reporting." Make sure your staff is telling you about both progress and problems. In too many companies and organizations I've heard employees say about management, "We don't know what's going on with them, and they don't know what's going on with us."

Do we have team spirit, a team attitude?

There must be mutual respect among team players.

Do we have team discipline?

Are all the players doing their best at what they do?

Are our strengths complementary?

Unity is the result of diversity, not uniformity. Imagine a football team on which every single player wanted to be the quarterback!

Do we have the top people available?

It's extremely difficult to form a team when half the players are missing or are not on a comparable and compatible level with the other members. It's like a football team on which some players are junior high or high school athletes, some are college players, and some play for the NFL. They could simply never have mutual respect—and, therefore, no team spirit.

Do we have a team "captain" responsible for final decisions?

Are you truly the team's leader? If not, who is?

Who can help us think and view our work more objectively?

What outsiders can give you needed objectivity and perspective about how well your team is doing?

Are we experienced in working as a team?

Are you doing more than just practicing? Are you playing the game?

Are we fatigued as a team?

Is it time for a break? Don't push the team so hard that they feel chronically fatigued.

REMEMBER

To keep building your team, return often to this chapter and ask yourself these questions:

- What is our team's inspirational dream?
- What is our practical masterplan?
- What training and tools do we need individually and as a team?
- What communications system do we need to keep the team on one track?
- Do we have team spirit, a team attitude?
- Do we have team discipline?
- Are our strengths complementary?
- Do we have the top people available?
- Do we have a team "captain" responsible for final decisions?
- Who can help us think and view our work more objectively?
- Are we experienced in working as a team?
- Are we fatigued as a team?

Knowing the right questions enhances your team-building skills and increases your leadership confidence.

CONCLUSION

In the year 2025 or 2050, when your children or grandchildren face various challenges and problems as they mature in leadership, I hope you will point them to this book. Its principles, I believe, are timeless; the questions in each chapter will serve the next generations just as well as they serve you today.

Use this book as a staff training resource. Read the chapters and discuss them together. Use it to build teamwork and to sharpen your collective leadership skills.

On the following pages you'll find a full list, in smaller type, of all the questions in each chapter. To keep the questions handy, clip or copy these pages, for instant reference when you need help in any of these thirty areas.

Finally, always remember that leadership is:

- knowing *what* to do next,
- knowing *why* that's important, and
- knowing how to bring appropriate *resources* to bear on the need at hand.

ASKING QUESTIONS

What? Why? When? Who? How? Where? How much?
Compared to what?
What's missing?
What is the ideal in this situation?
What would my five closest friends advise?
What lingering questions do I have?

ATTRACTIVENESS

THE INNER YOU
Do I have a positive attitude?
Am I self-centered or others-centered?
Do I really love people?
Do I encourage others?
Do I ask others the right questions?

THE OUTER YOU
What can I learn from others whose appearance I admire?
Does my appearance or image match my position?
Do I have enough energy to be attractive?

YOUR DREAMS
Do I have a future focus?

Do I really see my personal appearance as one of the best investments I can make in life?

BALANCE

Can I identify the specific areas in which I am experiencing imbalance?
To which of the seven basic areas of life have I been giving too much time, energy, and/or money?
Which area(s) have I been neglecting?
In which area(s) do I feel the most pressure, and why?
What three specific steps can I take to correct the imbalance I feel today?
What will be the unwanted result if I continue living with imbalance in my life?
Am I willing to pay the price it will take to become balanced?
To what (or whom) have I devoted the majority of my life energy?
Who or what would benefit most if my life regained a sense of balance? And who or what would lose most?
Who can help me restore my sense of life balance?

CHANGE

What is the context of the change?
What things never change?
What are the logical versus the psychological aspects of this change?
What are the advantages of the change?
Am I changing too much too fast? Should I allow this change?
Is this change temporary or permanent?
Is my attitude toward change right? Do I have the right appreciation for it?
What negative aspects of this change need creative problem solving?

COMMUNICATION

Who is my audience?
If I were to write a speech that captured fully the way my audience will most likely respond to what I'm communicating, what would the speech say?
What will most strongly influence my audience to accept my communication?
What will most strongly influence them to reject the communication?
What are my audience's five most predictable points of resistance?
What will be their three most likely misconceptions about my idea?
What are the facts involved? And what are the benefits related to each of those facts?
Why does my audience need to hear this message?
Would I agree with the idea if someone else tried to communicate it to me? Why or why not?
Am I making the message irresistible? What are the value and price considerations?
How can I visualize—tangibly or with word pictures—the rightness, the value, and the uniqueness of my message?

CONFIDENCE

In the situation that gives me anxiety and a lack of confidence, am I being too self-centered?
What realistically is the worst thing that could happen in this situation?
Who can I call for help in this situation?
Who are the friends who will love me regardless of whether I win or lose in this situation and in life?
In what area do I have a feeling of expertise?
What are my primary strengths, gifts, and talents?
What is my greatest strength?
What am I doing when I feel best about myself?
In what area of life do I have a natural interest in growing personally?
What's the focus of my life?

CREATIVITY

Do I have an attitude of readiness for creativity?
In the area in which I want to apply creativity, what is the need or problem?
Should I start from scratch to find an original solution for this need? Or is there a model or example I can follow?
How can I expand my perspective?
Is this need or problem really worth a lot of time?
How do I feel about the problem or need?
Has someone already solved this problem?
Who else could help me creatively think through this problem?
Could this solution be a really "Big Winner"?

DECISION MAKING

What are the five to ten most relevant, proven facts in this situation? And what are the fundamental assumptions I'm making about this situation?
How will this decision impact all the people involved?
What will be the long-term impact of this decision?
What legal, moral, or ethical concerns are involved in this decision?
Have I written down the basic issues involved in this decision?
What Mind-Stretcher Questions should I ask about this decision?
What are the trends related to this decision?
What other lingering questions do I have?

DELEGATING

Exactly *what* needs to be done?
Why does it need to be done?
When does it need to be done?
Who is the best person to do it?
How well must it be done?
How much budget is available for getting it done?
What training is needed for doing the task?
What reports do I need from the person who does it?
Who else may need to be aware of this assignment?
If it isn't done, what difference will it make?

DEPRESSION

Why am I depressed?
What specific things are weighing heavily on me today?
Am I angry at anyone?
Am I physically or mentally fatigued?
Have I been experiencing too much change too fast?
Am I seeing my situation with a long-term perspective?
Do I have clear and meaningful goals for the future?
What milestones in my past can cheer me up at this time?
What friend can I call to cheer me up at this time?
What positive, specific step can I take right now—no matter how small?
Do I need to "get away"?
To whom could I offer a meaningful gift?

DISCIPLINE

Do I have clear goals that are pulling me into the future?
Do I truly understand *why* I want to achieve these goals? And are these reasons constantly before me, for my inspiration?
Am I growing personally?
Is discipline missing in a certain area of my life? Why?
If discipline is missing in a certain area of my life, what are the possible or probable consequences if I don't restore or develop it?
Can I stay disciplined even when no one else notices?
How can I approach discipline in a step-by-step, achievable manner?
Who can I team up with for mutual encouragement?

DREAMING

What goal or cause or dream do I believe in deeply enough to die for?
What single need do I care most strongly about today?
What am I uniquely equipped and positioned to accomplish?
What are the long-term implications of accomplishing my dream?
What if my dream is a hundred times more successful than I plan?
Have I asked myself the Mind-Stretcher Questions?
Could someone else with an objective viewpoint help me see possibilities that I have been missing?
What successful models from the past may have something to say to me now?

FAILURE

Did I fail because of another person, because of my situation, or because of myself?
Did I actually fail, or did I simply fall short of an unrealistically high standard?
Where did I succeed, as well as "fail"?
What lessons have I learned?
Am I grateful for this experience?
How can I turn the failure into success?
Practically speaking, where do I go from here?
Who else has "failed" in this way before, and how can they help me?
How can my experience help others someday to keep from failing?

FATIGUE

How can I get an extra ten hours of sleep as soon as possible?
What things are weighing heavily on my shoulders?
Do I have clear, meaningful, and achievable goals?
Is my focus in life on *efficiency* (doing things right) or *effectiveness* (doing the right things)?
Am I in good physical condition?
Am I living on "natural" energy or "forced" energy?
Do I feel I am growing personally?
How can I approach my future work one step at a time?
What responsibilities can I delegate to others?
What Mind-Stretcher Questions should I be asking?

FIRING

Does this person clearly understand the role, goals, responsibilities, and standards for his or her position?
Why is the person not performing adequately?
What would be the benefits of having this person stay in the position?
What would be the difficulties associated with having this person stay in the position?
What psychological dynamics are involved in this person's staying or leaving?
Can this person be transferred to a different position? If so, what would be the associated advantages and difficulties?
How do I feel about this person? What feelings about the person are other team members experiencing?
Am I committed to this person's success?
What further questions must be answered before I will know whether he or she should go or stay?
What recognition does this person deserve?

GOAL SETTING

What needs do I care most deeply about meeting?
What is my life focus?
Why am I here? (What is my *purpose?*)
In what three to seven areas will I continue to concentrate my energy over the next five to ten years? (What are my *objectives?*)
What three specific and measurable things will I do this year in each area of my objectives? (What are my *goals?*)
Why do I want to accomplish these objectives and goals?
What will happen if I do *not* reach my goals?
Do I need to set goals that are more realistically attainable?
Who can help me be accountable for my goals?
How will I reward myself when I reach each goal?

INFLUENCING

What do I consider to be the three most important decisions to be made by other people in the near future?
Why do I want to influence these particular decisions?
Who will actually be making these decisions? And how can I influence them?
Am I committed to the best interests of these people? And how can I communicate that commitment?
What facts should these people be aware of before making these decisions?
Have I done my homework?
What are the value/price considerations in these decisions?
Who else wants to influence these decisions?
How can I invest money wisely to provide influence?
How will these decisions affect each person involved?

MASTERPLANNING

Who are we trying to serve, and what needs are we meeting? (Market)
Do we have the right people at the top to accomplish our goals? (Leadership)
Whose advice do we need in order to succeed? (Counsel)
Exactly what are we going to do short range, mid-range, and long range? (Direction)
Who will be responsible for what? And who will be responsible for whom? (Organization)
What are our expected expenses and income? (Cash)
Are we on target? (Reporting)
How can we effectively make known what we're doing? (Communication)
Are we seeing the quality we expect or demand from ourselves? (Evaluating)
How can we keep improving in the critical aspects of this project or service? (Refining)

MONEY

Am I generating adequate income?
Am I controlling expenses so that I have cash reserves?
Am I accounting for taxes?
Do I have a tangible picture—using graphs or charts—of the financial context for future decisions?
When you face a pressing financial decision, ask:
From whom should I seek counsel?
Should I wait to make this decision until I'm more objective about it?
Can I afford to lose all this money?
Exactly *why* am I making this decision?
Is this the right time to take this financial step?

MOTIVATING YOURSELF

Do I have clear, meaningful, and achievable goals?
WHY am I doing what I am doing?
In what areas of my life am I growing personally?
Am I fatigued?
What demotivators can I get rid of?
Is my life focused on giving or getting?
What needs do I most want to do something about this year?
Is my career path clearly in view?
What difference am I really making?

MOTIVATING OTHERS

What are this person's three greatest strengths?
What are this person's three most critical short-term decisions?
What are this person's top three measurable goals for the next month?
What are this person's top three measurable goals for the next two years?
What are the three major obstacles facing this person?
What are the three major resources this person can bring to bear on his situation?
What are this person's fears?
What are this person's dreams?
What could this person do if he or she had access to significantly more resources?
How can I help this person grow personally?

PEOPLE BUILDING

Do I know how to love unconditionally?
Do I really believe that:
 no one wants to fail?
 people do what makes sense to them?
 people who seem lazy really aren't (they simply haven't been properly motivated)?
 everyone wants to grow personally?
 everyone wants to make an important difference?
Do I encourage, appreciate, affirm, and recognize people?
Am I truly building people, or merely building my own dream and using people to do it?
Do I care enough to confront people when they really need it?
Am I listening to people with more than my ears—am I hearing more than their words?
Do I round out the "flat sides" of my staff?
Am I helping my staff members develop their greatest strengths?
Do I understand the true long-term potential of each of my staff members?
Do my staff members know I want them to reach their fullest personal potential?
Do I know what position each of my staff members would like to attain in the next five years? And am I helping each one to grow into it?

PERSONAL ORGANIZATION

Do I have a to-do list that works for me?
Do I have a calendar that works for me?
Do I have quick access to addresses and phone numbers?
Do I have a filing system that works for me?
Do I have a "Positive Progress List"?
Do I regularly set aside time on my calendar for personal organization? And do I keep these appointments with myself?
What three tools could help make me more effective?
Do I have a "Future File"?

PRESSURE

What specific things are weighing heavily on my shoulders today?
What three decisions are the most pressing today?
Am I getting proper rest?
If I'm overcommitted, how did happen?
Have I set unrealistically high goals for myself?
Am I trying to be perfect?
Who can help me relieve this pressure?
Can money help relieve this pressure?

PRIORITIZING

If I could achieve only three measurable goals this year, what would they be?
What are the top six things I want to accomplish in the next three months?
If I could choose only three things to accomplish today, what would they be?
What are all the things I need to accomplish in the next seven days? And how would I rate their importance?
What items on my to-do list am I truly committed to doing? And what items are only things I would like to get done but am not committed to?
What things on my list can be delegated to someone else?
What things on my list can be postponed?
What things on my list can I safely decide not to do at all?
Do I need a friend to help me look objectively at my priorities?

PROBLEM SOLVING

How would I prioritize the problems I face today?
In a single sentence, what is the problem?
How is my personal balance or imbalance affecting my ability to solve this problem?
What are the facts related to this problem?
Why does the problem exist?
What are the three greatest resources I can bring to bear on this problem?
Who can help me solve this problem?
Should I spend more money to reduce the time needed to solve this problem?
Of all the potential solutions to this problem, which one has the greatest potential to be right? And which one involves the lowest risk?
What policy would keep this problem from recurring?

RECRUITING

Exactly what is the job that needs to be done?
How much can and will I pay for this position?
When a strong candidate is under consideration, ask:
- Have I checked the right references?
- Should this person be given tests or inventories?
- Would I want someone I love to work for this person? Why or why not?
- What lingering questions do I have about this person?
- If I feel confident this person can do the job, why do I feel that way?
- Am I in favor of hiring this person because of his or her obvious strengths or because of a lack of any glaring weaknesses?
- What else should I ask this person before making a final hiring decision?
- Once a hiring decision has been made, what assumptions have I made that need to be spelled out in writing?

REPORTING

Questions for Your Staff:
- What *decisions* do you need from me?
- What *problems* are you facing on which my input is needed?
- What *plans* am you making that we have not discussed?
- What *program* have you made?
- How are you doing *personally?*

Questions for You:
- Are each staff member's top three annual goals clearly understood?
- How frequently is a report needed from each staff member?
- What visuals—graphs and charts, etc.—need to be regularly presented and updated by staff members?
- What information from my staff do I need to pass on to my manager or board?

RISK TAKING

What's the worst thing that could happen?
What's the best thing that could happen?
Is it worth the risk?
Have I sought proper counsel?
Do I fully understand the process and context of the situation?
Have I asked the key Mind-Stretcher Questions?
Have I established definite criteria for any risk I take?
How can I break down the project or task into sequential steps in order to minimize risk, yet still keep it going?
Have I established test milestones: go/no-go points?
What risks am I taking by *not* acting in the situation?
What research could check my assumptions about the risk?
Am I in agreement with the team about our basic assumptions regarding this risk?

TEAM BUILDING

What is our team's inspirational dream?
What is our practical masterplan?
What training and tools do we need individually and as a team?
What communications system do we need to keep the team on one track?
Do we have team spirit, a team attitude?
Do we have team discipline?
Are our strengths complementary?
Do we have the top people available?
Do we have a team "captain" responsible for final decisions?
Who can help us think and view our work more objectively?
Are we experienced in working as a team?
Are we fatigued as a team?

LEADERSHIP RESOURCES

FROM
MASTERPLANNING GROUP

The following field-tested resources are listed alphabetically for easy reference.

Asking to Win!

This booklet (part of our Pocket Confidence series) goes in your suit coat pocket, briefcase, or purse. It contains one hundred profound questions—ten questions to ask in each of the following situations:

1. *Asking* profound personal questions and avoiding "small talk"
2. *Brainstorming* your way out of a mental "rut" and maximizing your finest ideas
3. *Career-ing* when you, or a friend, are considering a career change

4. *Deciding* when a risky, pressurized, costly decision needs to be made
5. *Interviewing.* Getting behind a person's smile and beyond her/his résumé
6. *Focusing* or refocusing your life
7. *Organizing* your life to maximize your time
8. *Parenting* to raise healthy balanced children
9. *Planning.* Masterplanning any organization or major project
10. *Solving* any problem faster, with a systematic problem-solving process

Whenever you have a tough situation, ask profound questions to get profound answers and make wise decisions. These booklets are packaged/priced reasonably enough for you to give to adult children, colleagues, friends, protégés, spouses, staff members, etc.

Career Change Questions/Lifework

30 Questions to Ask before Making Any Major Career Change

This series of thirty questions comes in handy anytime you are thinking about the possibility of making a career change. Also, friends in transition are helped. You may hand them the thirty questions, and they could take hours to answer them; however, they will come back with well thought-out answers. These questions save you hours of uncertainty.

Is your current position "Just a Job," your next "Career Move," or your "Lifework"? If you are uncertain, these profoundly simple ideas can help. This is priority reading for any reevaluating person ages twenty-five to sixty. A proven resource!

Event Planning (Successful) Checklist

by Ed Trenner

This comprehensive three-hundred-point checklist can *cut your planning time in half*, especially if you are new to "special events." This checklist is designed for those who receive great pleasure from precision and for those who have yet to experience it. The three-hundred-point checklist helps you keep from overlooking an obvious question and finding "egg on your face" at the event. This is a practical, proven, easy-to-use resource!

Executive Evaluation—135

Have you ever wanted a comprehensive evaluation checklist for telling a staff member exactly how he or she is doing, on a one to ten scale, in everything from bad breath to decision making?

This is it—135 dimensions in all. This is an ideal annual tool for you to use with those close to you. And, if you like, let them evaluate you. This list helps maximize your staff evaluation and communication ability while concentrating on the positive.

Focusing Your Life

Often life, even for a leader, gets foggy, confused, and overwhelming. *Focusing Your Life* simplifies life!

Focusing Your Life is a simple, step-by-step process you learn in about three hours, which helps "clear the fog" and keeps you focused for the rest of your life. This great, personal retreat guide helps you reflect on your future!

Focusing Your Life has been used by more than four thousand people to help form a crystal-clear direction in life. Let this resource help you *focus* and *simplify* your life.

Heart to Heart Marriage Series

by Bobb and Cheryl Biehl

Whether you're about to pop the question or popped it years ago, answering the questions in the Heart to Heart Marriage Series will be a great way to communicate with your mate. Asking each other these fresh questions can and will identify possible trouble spots in your relationship and show you how to deal with them before they become marriage threatening.

Each of the books contains approximately 250 questions stimulating many heart-to-heart conversations, covering the seven basic areas of life. In addition, each book has detailed steps for resolving disagreements.

These are wonderful gifts for any friend whose marriage could benefit from a little more heart-to-heart communication. They also are a perfect counseling supplement! Assign any couple the appropriate book and have them spend several hours discussing the questions. There is a place in each book to mark the questions that are "major sticking points." The couple then comes to you with a handful of clearly defined differences. These four books can literally save you hundreds of hours per year of counseling time.

Premarriage Questions: Getting to "Really Know" Your Lifemate-to-Be

These are the heart-to-heart questions you ask before you say "I do" to make sure this is the right person for you. It is hard to break up any relationship, but it is far better to break an engagement than a marriage.

Most couples find that they have far more in common than they had even realized. The handful of major disagreements can be discussed before the marriage to see if they are "engagement breakers" or if they are just uncomfortable differences. If you have any doubts at all about your upcoming marriage at all but can't put your finger on the source of the doubts, or if you just want to make sure this is the lifemate for you, this book can help!

If you know someone who is about to be married and you feel/think/know that the marriage could be a disaster—but you can't say so or it would make the person want to get married even more—this is a great gift. An effective way for the person to see how the marriage would actually work is to ask these questions. It is ideal to let the person come to his or her own conclusion that being married to a person who thinks like this would be a terrible mistake. *Premarriage Questions* is an appropriate gift for any friend.

Newly Married Questions: Making the Most of Your Honeymoon Year

If you are in your first few years of marriage, especially your first year, and you sense you have a few fundamental differences, this book can really help identify these points before they grow into marriage threatening issues. It is far easier to address these questions while you are still in the "honeymoon" period of your marriage. These questions spark wonderful fireside chats and make a perfect wedding gift supplement.

Anniversary Questions: Keeping Your Marriage Healthy and Sizzling

Ask each other these heart-to-heart questions if you want to maximize your great marriage. These questions can also add quite specific definition to any differences that are under the surface before they become major problems.

This book freshens, rekindles, and maximizes your heart-to-heart communications. It's great for a long weekend together, long road trips, or vacation conversation, and it also makes interesting meal conversation if you tend to run out of things to talk about when the children are gone—great in the early empty-nester years.

A very appropriate gift for any friend's anniversary, first to seventieth!

Pre-remarriage Questions: Helping You Start Again

Do you have certain delicate questions you would desperately like to ask your fiancee but you find asking them "out of the blue" is quite uncomfortable. By systematically going through all of the questions in this book, even the most delicate questions can be approached with "the next question is . . . ."

Most couples in the process of marrying again because of death or divorce very appropriately want desperately to avoid making a mistake in this marriage. If your first marriage was the best marriage of the century or was one of the worst disasters of the decade, these heart-to-heart questions let you enter your next marriage with your eyes "wide open"!

Leadership Confidence (tape series)

Approximately 3,500 people have completed the Leadership Confidence series. A wise, proven investment in your own future, this series is a lifelong reference covering thirty essential leadership areas including:

- How to cope with change, depression, failure, fatigue, and pressure.
- How to become more attractive, balanced, confident, creative, disciplined, and motivated.
- How to develop skills in asking, dreaming, goal setting, prioritizing, risk taking, influencing, money managing, personal organization, problem solving, decision making, and communicating.
- How to become more effective in delegating, firing, reporting, team building, people building, recruiting, masterplanning, and motivating.

The series consists of a 166-page outline in a three-ring notebook and eight audio cassettes.

Masterplanning Your Church

This complete notebook and eight-hour audio cassette tape series will not replace private consulting. However, if your church membership is under five hundred or your organization has less than twenty employees, the place to start is with this resource!

This series presents the same notebook and planning process that our consulting associates have refined in day-to-day practice over the past eighteen years to help clients develop their masterplans. A masterplan helps the board, the senior executive, and the executive staff work together in a unified way.

The series is available as a hardback book, or with eight hours of audio cassette tapes and a complete notebook.

Masterplanning Arrow

The 24" x 36" Masterplanning Arrow with instructions on the back is now available without ordering the entire Masterplanning process.

Memories Book

A written bridge linking generations . . . . Are your parents, grandparents, favorite aunts, uncles, or mentors still living? Then, *Memories* is an ideal gift. Written memories become family heirlooms for your children's children and are guaranteed to become priceless with the passage of time. *Memories* contains more than five hundred memory-jogging questions to help your loved one relive and write about her or his life's milestones.

Memories is a beautiful album-type book with padded covers and a binding that opens widely for easy writing. It is designed to last hundreds of years because it is printed on museum-quality, acid-free paper. *Memories* takes time to complete, filling lonely hours with happy remembrances, while creating a precious family heirloom. It is a "boomerang" gift! You give it to your loved one this year, and he or she fills it with memories over the next one to fifty years. It then returns to you as an heirloom for you and your children and for your children's children. *Memories* is quite an affordable gift for any loved one.

Mentoring (book)

Confidence in Finding a Mentor and Becoming One

If you would like to be a mentor or find a mentor, but don't know where to start, this is it! This book explains clearly and completely what mentors do and don't do, the nature of the mentor/protégé relationship, the most common roadblocks to effective mentoring, and much more.

Mentoring is an invaluable way of teaching skills, traditions, and cultural nuances that can't be captured in the classroom. It helps you (as protégé) reach your full potential, and gives you (as mentor) the satisfaction of seeing your experience and ideals carried forward to the next generation. Mentoring is something anyone *can* do but not everyone *should* do. This book shows you that being a successful mentor doesn't require perfection, and finding a mentor is probably much easier than you think. Mentoring can make a major difference in your life.

Mentoring is the "lynch pin" connecting this generation of leadership to the next. If you have been praying about a way to have your life make quite a significant difference, mentoring may be your life ministry!

Mentoring (booklet)

How to Find a Mentor and How to Become One
by Bobb Biehl and Glen Urquhart
Without a mentor, a person often feels underpowered, as if not living up to her or his true potential. A mentoring relationship can easily add 30 to 50 percent extra "life and leadership horsepower" to any person. This booklet gives you many useful how-to steps for forming a mentoring relationship and answers practical mentoring questions with life-proven answers.

Mentoring Men Video

At a Promise Keepers' conference, Bobb Biehl spoke to approximately four thousand men on the subject of mentoring men. Now you can watch this video in your men's group. It will help your men understand mentoring and how to get started in the mentoring process—an extremely stimulating video for a men's retreat.

Mentoring Wisdom

This volume contains approximately two hundred quotable leadership principles, rules of thumb, and observations that are key to generating creative ideas and gaining objective perspective!

Add your own principles over the next twenty to thirty years. Build it for a lifetime and then pass it on to help all who look to you for leadership—children, grandchildren, and protégés.

Midlife Storm

by Bobb Biehl

Here's how to avoid a "midlife crisis"! Just because you or your mate are beginning to ask a few midlife questions does not automatically mean that you are experiencing the dreaded "midlife crisis."

There are three distinctly different midlife phases: reevaluation, crisis, and dropout. This book addresses each of the three phases with specific step-by-step instructions on how to avoid the pain and confusion of the midlife years; or if you are already there, how to get out and get on with the rest of your life.

This book contains a crystal-clear "midlife map" (worth the price of the book) which helps guide you successfully through the very dangerous midlife years.

On My Own Handbook

by Bobb Biehl

This is a proven "growth group" book for young teenagers, college students, young professionals, and newlyweds—an ideal graduation gift!

If you have been increasingly concerned about your high school or college student's readiness to face the "real world," this book has been written for your son or daughter.

In the past fifteen-plus years, Bobb Biehl has consulted with more than one hundred presidents of organizations and companies. The principles in this book are the same ones he teaches presidents, but written at a precollege level. If your son or daughter is eager to learn and enjoys reading, this may be the perfect gift—*before* they leave home!

Many adults have said that they wish their parents had taught them these principles before they started off "on their own." Parents, as well as students, benefit from these extremely fundamental leadership principles, which will stay with your son or daughter for a lifetime. And they likely will pass many on to their children's children. This is help for a lifetime.

Pastoral Search Process

This eighteen-step staff search process can help you find exactly the senior pastor, associate pastor, worship leader, youth director, or staff person that you need! Literally, it also can save you thousands of dollars and years of trying to correct one single hiring mistake!

When hiring, this process is worth its "weight in gold." No one can absolutely guarantee you will attract and select the right person, but this systematic approach will significantly enhance your wisdom in the selection process.

Presidential Profile

- Am I cut out to be a president? How would I rate myself as a president?
- Where do I need to grow to be ready to be president someday?
- Which of the candidates we are interviewing to be our next president gets the highest rating on the presidential profile?
- How would we rate our current president?

If you have been asking yourself any of the above questions, this easy to understand (1-10 scale) profile can be a proven guide for your reflections and your team's discussions or evaluations. This easy-to-read paper helps identify, evaluate, and define your strengths and growth areas as you get ready to be a world-class president.

Process Charting: How to Do It!

Process charting possibly is the most valuable and least understood skill in leadership today. A clear understanding of process charting provides a framework for fundamental organizational components such as policy, procedure, problem solving, predicting impact, staff communications, curriculum development, logic checking, filing, monitoring, program overview, program transfer, new staff orientation, and time lines. Understanding process charting is also a key element of quality control and transferability!

Role Preference Inventory

The *Role Preference Inventory* (sixth edition, seventeenth printing since 1980) is a proven way of understanding yourself better. In simple language, it lets you tell your spouse, your friends, or your colleagues:

- "What makes you tick!"
- "What turns you on!"
- "What burns you out!"

The *Role Preference Inventory* clarifies what you really want to do, not what you have to do, have done the most, or think others expect of you. It is the key to understanding personal fulfillment and is an affordable way of building strong team unity by predicting team chemistry.

This profoundly simple, self-scoring, self-interpreting inventory is the key to selecting the right person for the right position, thus helping avoid costly hiring mistakes.

Senior Pastor Profile

by Bobb Biehl and John Maxwell

For the past twenty-plus years, Bobb Biehl has been consulting with senior pastors and helping turn their dreams into reality. For the past twenty-plus years, John Maxwell has been a successful senior pastor and has inspired thousands of pastors as a teacher/speaker. This series combines some of their finest insights into what it takes to make it as a senior pastor.

The Senior Pastor Profile has several applications, including:

- Evaluating a current senior pastor to see what's missing or where growth areas are recommended
- Analyzing a candidate for a senior pastor position to determine his areas of strength and needed growth
- Helping a person who wants to someday be a senior pastor identify the areas in which he needs to grow, so he will be ready when opportunity knocks

This checklist has been developed from literally thousands of hours of interaction with senior pastors, but it is not to be seen as 100 percent complete. If it can give you 80 percent to 95 percent of what you're looking for in spotting strengths, problems, or defining growth areas, its mission will have been accomplished.

As you go through this profile, rate yourself, or your current candidate, by each attribute on a scale of one to ten with ten being a great strength and one being a major weakness.

Senior Pastor Profile contains six audio cassettes with more than six hours of very candid conversation about what it really takes to be a great senior pastor according to the combined wisdom of Bobb Biehl and John Maxwell; a workbook, and a scoring system to help you identify the areas in which you need to/want to grow in order to reach your full potential as a senior pastor.

Strategy Work Sheets (11" x 17")

This quick, systematic, step-by-step tool helps you think through a solid success strategy for each of your goals. Use these sheets to ask each staff member to draft a strategy for turning each major goal into a realistic plan. *Strategy Work Sheets* helps you spot problems in basic thinking and strategy before those problems become costly. Includes twenty-four (11" x 14") sheets for use with your team.

"Ten Most Wanted" Cards

(Bulletin Inserts)

This profoundly simple card (fifteenth printing since 1989) unlocks a refreshing new excitement about *evangelism* without putting believers under the "guilt pile." Just the word *evangelism* throws many Christians into a panic. At the same time, it is a biblical mandate. This bulletin insert explains how to encourage each believer to focus on attracting his or her ten most wanted relatives, friends, and acquaintances to faith in Christ sometime in their lifetime. This profoundly simple tool is easy to use, inexpensive to try, and extremely effective! It is the ideal supplement to any sermon or series on evangelism.

Why You Do What You Do

by Bobb Biehl

This book is a result of more than 21,000 hours of behind-the-defenses experiences with some of the finest (emotionally healthy) Christian leaders of our generation. This model was developed to maximize "healthy" people with a few emotional "mysteries" still unanswered!

- Why do I have a phobic fear of failure, rejection, or insignificance?
- Why am I so "driven" to be admired, recognized, appreciated, secure, respected, or accepted?
- Why am I an enabler, leader, promoter, rescuer, controller, or people pleaser?
- Why am I a perfectionist, workaholic, or "withdrawer" from tough situations?
- Why are pastors vulnerable to affairs? Where am I the most vulnerable to temptation? How do I guard against temptation?
- Why do I have such a hard time relating to my parents when I love them so much? Why do they sometimes seem like such children?

These and other "emotional mysteries" can be understood and resolved in the silence of your own heart without years of therapy. (Hardback book, 241 pages.)

Wisdom for Men

by Bobb Biehl

Wisdom for Men contains life principles combined with parallel Scriptures to give wise perspective on many topics. It is in an easy-to-read format and is great relaxation reading—stretch and relax at the same time. Need a gift for someone's birthday or for Christmas, Father's Day, or graduation, etc.? This would make a great one!

Writing Your First Book

by Bobb Biehl and Mary Beshear, Ph.D.

If you have been wanting to write a book for years but still haven't actually started a manuscript, let this be your starting point! This is a skeleton outline—no complicated, sophisticated theory or double talk. It is just a bare bones, easy-to-follow, step-by-step checklist to becoming a royalty-receiving author. A wise investment in your own future!

For Additional Information Write To:

Masterplanning Group International
Box 952499
Lake Mary, FL 32795

Please send me the following (free of charge):

[ ] Masterplanning Group's resource catalog
[ ] Consulting information
[ ] Speaking information

My name ______________________________
Title__________________________________
Organization ___________________________
Address _______________________________
City ______________ State _____ Zip_______
Daytime telephone (_________) ___________
Fax (________) _________________________

To reach Masterplanning Group by telephone:

Executive offices: 1-407-330-2028
Fax: 1-407-330-4134
Ordering materials: 1-800-443-1976